Heavenly Match

A Spirit Guide

and a

Deep Trance Channel

Tell Their True Stories

of

How and Why They Met

April Crawford

and

VERONICA

A Heavenly Match

April Crawford and VERONICA

Title: **Heavenly Match: A Spirit Guide and a Deep Trance Channel Tell Their True Stories of How and Why They Met**

Authors: April Crawford, VERONICA

Publisher: Connecting Wave
2629 Foothill Blvd.
Unit # 353
La Crescenta, CA 91214
www.ConnectingWave.com

ISBN: 978-0-9823269-3-0

For Author Information:
www.AprilCrawford.com

Other books via April Crawford:
www.AprilCrawfordBooks.com

Book Design: Allen Crawford

For Permissions: Publisher@ConnectingWave.com

Contents

CONTENTS

Introduction

I have attended virtually every single in-person full body open deep trance channeling session (but not the telephone consultations) held via April Crawford.

Because April is an "Open" deep trance channel, these sessions have involved not only many different nonphysical beings, but many types and levels of nonphysical beings.

However, in this book the Entity we call VERONICA tells her personal story, as does April. Accordingly this introduction is mostly limited to the sessions and experiences with VERONICA and April, as told by each of them individually in the following pages.

Here, I wish only to convey a few particulars about how this book came to be.

Introduction

You will soon note that this book is made up of many short, sometimes very short, numbered chapters. This was in some sense due to the fact that in most cases, the chapters represent a single writing session by either VERONICA or April.

Also, as an editorial choice, I happen to prefer short chapters, perhaps because when I read, I always like to stop after finishing a chapter. With short chapters, especially if you read in bed, opportunities to do so abound before getting too tired and starting to drift just to get to the next chapter.

There were also some arbitrarily made editorial choices to add certain punctuation, mostly commas, but also not to add some, including semi-colons or colons, particularly with VERONICA's writing.

For example, when you speak with VERONICA (or anyone for that matter), they will often follow up a thought with a short sentence that if written instead of being spoken, would involve a semi-colon or a colon to finish the previous sentence. However, I personally don't like those particular punctuation marks in a narrative book because for me they interrupt the flow or energy of what is being said.

Also., for example, while it is usually correct to put a comma after the phrase "of course", since that is not how VERONICA or April talk, I did not add commas in every "proper" place. If you read the book as if VERONICA and April were talking with you, or if you speak the sentence out loud, it may help those with the red pens to be more comfortable :-D.

I was also informed separately by both VERONICA and April that the chapters of this book would be written in no particular order. In other words, outside of the normal timeline. At first I wondered how I could possibly arrange them so that they followed a traditional timeline. However, once they were all completed, I realized that the weaving in and out of a straight line flow of time worked, at least for me.

While this book could have, in my humble opinion, easily been written in a few months, in actuality it required almost two years to complete.

Introduction

Why? Surely VERONICA at least could have written several sessions per day every day without missing a beat.

Well, the physical reality is that both VERONICA and April maintain a considerable schedule. VERONICA consults one-on-one, mostly via phone, with clients from almost every country in the world, every day, several hours a day, seven days a week, 365 days a year (except one or two national holidays in the USA). It should go without saying that this also requires the physical body and the agreement of April to be present, so those particular physical times are also not available to April for other things.

In addition, VERONICA writes two columns for the weekly *"Inner Whispers"* newsletter: (www.InnerWhispers.net), which by definition also requires the presence and physical time of April Crawford's body. Further, I have many of my own personal sessions with VERONICA *and others*, some of whom are writing their own books. All of this takes physical time. April Crawford also has a regular physical life, married, pets, home, family, etc. So, book writing is done catch as catch can.

There are a few things that I will mention about April's recollections as related in the following pages. First and foremost is that April was generally not there, as she goes completely "out" and VERONICA and the others come completely in. By completely, I mean completely.

Accordingly, my memory of the actual sessions is substantially more expansive than April's (but not VERONICA's). For example, when April says that VERONICA let her listen into a few sessions, the few should be taken to mean very few. Also, none of the others, the many others that come through, have granted April that opportunity.

Even to this day, April routinely asks me after a deep trance channeling session, "Did anyone come through?". This is frequent question, even though they did, in a several hour continuous sometimes intense deep trance channeling sessions, where many of them get up and explore our house and the objects within, particularly if their last physical incarnation

Introduction

was in an earlier time historically, or if they are just particularly curious. The latter is often the case with the scientific types.

Another thing I wish to mention is that this book represents something new for us.

This is the first book that tells full length true stories as opposed to direct short messages from VERONICA or very short stories from those who have actually "died". This will be the first in a series of such full length memoirs, each told by a very highly evolved nonphysical being. Several of such beings have already asked to reserve a place in the book writing queue, and two of those have actually started writing *their* true multiple life and multidimensional stories.

For those who are interested in such things, I will add some additional background from my perspective in the Appendix. For now, please understand that this is all true, and all real.

VERONICA has consulted with literally thousands of individuals over the years. You can also see examples of VERONICA speaking on YouTube on the *"Inner Whispers" TV* Channel on YouTube or via www.InnerWhispersTV.com.

Best wishes,

-Allen

Facilitator for April Crawford

Administrator for VERONICA

About April Crawford

April Crawford is a natural Full Body Open Deep Trance Channel and Spirit Medium. These are relatively rare.

Because April is able to be completely open and without any fear of the process whatsoever, the nonphysical Entities and guides who come through are able to <u>totally</u> integrate with the physical, while at the same time not blending at all with April's personality. They therefore have <u>full</u> physical and emotional control during their "visits".

This allows zero distortion or "coloring" by April, and also allows them to walk around the room, go out for a walk in the night air, keep their eyes wide open when they speak, and even eat or drink if they wish (but most choose not to).

About April Crawford

These physical abilities are one of the things that allow VERONICA... the name we have given to the highly evolved nonphysical Entity and guide that is a co-author of this book... to give readings and have long, fully interactive conversations over a speakerphone, and even to write in longhand herself (not automatic writing), or type on a computer keyboard, and even use a computer mouse or computer touch screen. In other words, everything that you can do in your body while you are in it.

You can see videos of VERONICA speaking while April Crawford is in deep trance at: www.AprilCrawford.com

April routinely allows many different Entities and Aspects of Entities to come through (this is what the word "open" means in the technical description), and they have a full range of motion and emotion. Some who are in-between physical lives, for example, have cried uncontrollably or expressed total joy when we advised them of certain things about their physical lives.

About VERONICA

The Spirit Guide that wrote "her" story is VERONICA.

"VERONICA", as we call "her", is an evolved nonphysical Entity and guide. "She" refers to herself as a nonphysical consciousness. VERONICA comes across as female energy when we consult with her, even though VERONICA has physically been both sexes and has told me that her favorite physical life was as a male in Bristol England.

VERONICA has enjoyed physical incarnation and has done so many times, which means that she has also experienced physical birth, and physical death many time. This experience helps her in her consultations with those currently incarnated.

About VERONICA

Of course this is in addition to VERONICA's ability to "read" the energy of any person physically living at the moment or not, any place or thing, and in addition to her many (very many) associates on the "other side" at all levels of evolution and expertise who help out with certain subjects from time to time.

(Note: Some other Entities and individuals in-between physical lives that come through April Crawford express themselves as male energies, so it is not because April is female that VERONICA expresses herself as female this time.)

You may wonder about VERONICA's name. Actually, it is a name we gave her many years ago.

When she first came through, it was rather amazing and rather dramatic (VERONIA was not the first to come through, but was certainly the most intense).

At that time, "she" did not give us a name when we asked, saying basically that, "Labels are not necessary." She went on to say that if we needed a label, that we could choose whatever name we wanted.

We chose the name "VERONICA", and it stuck. Now, even other nonphysical beings who visit via April Crawford's Open Deep Trance Channeling know exactly who VERONICA is if we mention her by that name. It seems that things get around in the cosmos rather quickly, and rather completely!

All of VERONICA's books and newsletter columns are either spoken or written by her in first, final, and only draft. There is never any editing of a single sentence or word. As facilitator, I (Allen) do sometimes arbitrarily add some punctuation, usually commas. Also, VERONICA almost never uses the word "and" when writing, instead always choosing the "+" or "&" symbols. I usually change these to the word "and".

-Allen

Facilitator for April Crawford

Administrator for VERONICA

"Everyone was always in awe and amazed with this energy they named 'VERONICA'. Since I had no memory, I had to go with what they told me."

-April Crawford

1

April Crawford

When I was a little girl... I have a clear memory of my parents taking me to the county fair. It was a big affair to those who lived there, especially to children who thrilled in the Midway full of rides. Of course there were farm animals, exhibits, and contests for the best cherry pie. A small town environment that in the 50's was a great place to grow up in.

My earliest memory of the fair though was not all the aforementioned. Nor the food. It was the log cabin that had been refurbished. It was called the Eby Cabin because it had sat on the Eby homestead for over one hundred years. The historical society had it moved to the fairgrounds and completely refurbished it with authentic décor.

I must have been about five the first time I walked into it. The interior seemed so familiar that it took my breath away. The smell of the wood transfixed me to the spot by the fireplace. Again, I was only five so the reaction was not one my parents were expecting.

I refused to move from the spot. My mother's hand grabbed mine tightly.

"Let's go April," she murmured under her breath.

I heard her but my gaze could not tear itself from the interior. I wanted to touch the table, the wood box, the oil lamp, and anything else that would continue the visions in my head.

I could hear wood being chopped from a distance, chickens clucking in the yard. A smell of food cooking also overwhelmed me. Mind you, there was no fire being stoked in the fireplace.

The feeling was that of "I am home".

My mom now irritated with my behavior began to pull me towards the door.

"I don't want to leave," I cried.

"Why not?" replied my mother, her hands now postured upon her hips.

"Come on April, let's go on the rides," chimed in my father, who had missed most of the exchange.

Both of them were dismayed that I had suddenly planted myself in this primitive log cabin.

All I knew was that I was home.

2

April Crawford

It took them quite a while to lure me out of there. It wasn't a carnival ride that finally dissuaded me. It was the promise that we could return later.

I did hold them to the promise.

Every year from that time forward I would insist upon a visit to that log cabin. I would lovingly touch the wood, running my fingers over the edges over and over. It was always with a longing that I never understood until much later.

Long after I left Michigan, my mother would still remark about my love for that log cabin. No other place touched me quite as deeply.

In school I developed a taste for history. Some locales more enticing than others, but a rustic log cabin always managed to send me into a swoon.

3

April Crawford

Growing up in a small town was always a benefit in my formative years. I was sent to a Catholic Grade School, following up with 4 years of high school at an all-girl Catholic Boarding School. I was a day student, but the traditional atmosphere made it more intense than a regular public school.

The building itself was built in the 1930's. A previous structure built in the 1800's burned down in 1926. I can remember feeling a deja vu when I walked down the halls. Of course at the time, I did not realize why.

We had study periods where we were often allowed to go to the library that was actually for the retired nuns. It was a bit more sophisticated than our high school library. I would go there simply for the adventure of it, for to get there a walk in an underground tunnel was needed.

It was a Friday afternoon when I stumbled upon the archive section where the history of the school was stored. I sat on the ground paging through old photos from the early 1900's. I was mesmerized by the look of everything. There was a moment of clarity when, as I was about to turn a page, it occurred to me that the next section was about May Day and its significance to the girls of that early time.

I was surprised to see photos of the students in their May Day Celebrations. I felt lost in it for a moment. To my complete shock, I saw a blurred picture of a girl holding a maypole ribbon. I couldn't see her face, but felt very familiar with it.

I stared at it for a long time, never really coming to a conclusion about it then. Now, I would venture to say it was a photo of myself in a past life.

Of course there is no proof, but in my experiences since then, I have found my instincts to be true.

4

April

I should also include the presence of dance in my life. Like a lot of little girls, growing up, in the sixties dance was an acceptable activity. These days, sports have become very popular, but in those times, girls did not play organized sports.

I remember the classes well. They were held in a church across town. My mother, a frustrated dancer herself, took me diligently every Friday. All dolled up in my leotard and tap shoes, I tippy toed through songs that I remember to this day.

I took to the classes gradually adding more as I grew older. The physical activity was stimulating, actually keeping me focused in my physical body. Not realizing at the time that others did not need assistance staying in their bodies, I found tap and ballet to be helpful.

My whole childhood was spent at the "barre", culminating in opening my own studio when I was just sixteen.

It helped that my mother had danced for she was really the brains behind the business. I taught, while she kept the books. It was a good partnership. One that lasted almost forty years.

Eventually in my early twenties, I went to Los Angeles to find out for myself how good of a dancer I really was. My mother kept the home fires burning by hiring other teachers to take my place at the studio. She always wanted me to come home, hoping that I would find the validation I need and return home to teach.

I was 23 when I arrived in LA, my time occupied by dance classes and auditions. Occasionally I would feel the same déjà vu's of my childhood, but they were firmly put out of my mind while concentrating on the next dance combination.

5

VERONICA

Attempting to comply with the denseness, we arrived at our first memory. They are indeed chronicles of experience often dismissed when reconvened soulfully.

Our reckoning for this verbiage is to define our energy linearly. Thus doing so, establish a conceivable declaration of intention.

One would ask our intent:

"Why do we now speak through a physical form, when our evolution has taken us far away from the physical reality?"

"What does it serve for those like ourselves to agree to such an arrangement?"

We say that all of you are on the same journey. Just further down the path are we.

A blending of many creates the voice you now hear. A harmony of experience, perception, and knowledge not so available when one begins the journey.

6

VERONICA

As we advanced energetically, others of different perspective joined until the number is no longer relevant.

It is the desire of our essence to assist others on the journey so that they know what is needed from them. A give and take of energy, the pulse of all who are conscious.

We now give so that others receive. With that, the chain continues until they themselves are eager to give back. We participate with pure thought and intention.

It is important to understand one's origin. The ability to apply the lesson truly imperative to the growth. We wish to share the beginnings of our relationship with the April Crawford.

We knew not of her whilst we were at the beginning stages of our own evolution. Nor did we incarnate with her. Having reached a pinnacle of understanding, we realized the time was upon us to participate in this fashion.

Seeking counsel from our own source and the universe, we reached out in the space, seeking a possible connection.

We found it.

The match energetically was perfect. A vehicle of openness that surpassed expectation. We thought it would be a highly evolved spiritual leader on the planet. Perhaps an energy like ourselves who had decided to take human form.

A vision was created in our thoughts. Reaching out in the mist, we found ourselves in the woman's form who let us in, but was not what we expected.

Truly it was a match, however, one should never prematurely come to conclusions. It was a woman called April. She was quite an experience.

7

April Crawford

"I could go into all the dramas of this time period, but maybe some time should be spent by defining me.

The love of dance became an obsession. The intense focus upon physical matters lessened the impact of spiritual incidents that were really forming my life.

Life from twenty three through thirty was filled with show business. A series of jobs filled my resume and I soon found myself continually employed. There was always the idea of never having what one would call a real job. It was a level of success as a dancer to not have to go that route.

Dance took me across the country, and to foreign countries and back. The more focused upon the physical I became, the more comfortable I felt. The feelings of déjà vu were superseded by the athletic abilities I had created with dance. Along the way, I became interested in other venues, but always returned to my dance roots.

A few times I was offered an acting role or two, but dismissed them as a lark. Dance was my mantra, and I stayed the course.

This lifestyle went on for many years. Along the way, a series of boyfriends presented themselves, of course all of them inappropriate, but dramatic just the same.

When I turned 30, I met a man who prompted the déjà vu's to begin all over again. His name was Michael, an assistant director on a film where I was hired to dance.

8

April Crawford

I spent a lot of time dancing during the next 10 years.   My escape from traditional Catholic upbringing kept me from pursuing any sort of religious participation.   I always used to tease my friends by saying I went to church six days a week for twelve years of school, so, I had enough time banked to last awhile.

So dance I did.   There was a magic to being in Hollywood.   I loved looking at all the old photographs from the 20's and 30's.   I tried to get to all the historical spots to see them for myself.   It was a hobby for me until I worked on the old MGM lot.

I was a dancer in the movie musical "Pennies From Heaven".   Again, long hours, sore muscles for weeks on end.   The first time I stepped into the commissary, I felt an odd sensation, like everything was in slow motion.   The hum of the lunch crowd, all of them dressed in costume for whatever they were working on suddenly shifted into the background. I felt the room as it was, seeing people who were from another place and time.

It lasted only a moment, but it impacted me a lot. I knew I had been there before. Of course I shrugged it off by the time I got back to the sound stage.

It returned while a line of us descended down a stairway. I knew then that I had been in a dance sequence from that 30's timeframe. That memory has stayed with me vividly since then.

Now, knowing what I know, I am sure I was some sort of chorus girl in the movies during the 1930 – 1940's. I've often wanted to research it, have never gotten around to it.

9

April Crawford

Since I spent so much time in a parochial school system, I tended to stay away from religious practices in my early adulthood.

I tried to live a good life, but going to church was not on my agenda. It wasn't until my early thirties that any sort of spiritual practices piqued my interest.

The year was 1983. I had landed a great job dancing in the musical "42'nd Street". It was considered a plum job because unlike other local dance jobs, it was going to last at least a year. Being used to having gigs that last a day, a week, or if lucky a month, this was a dream come true.

A dancer lives a fairly nomadic life, unless one is willing to teach instead of perform. So having the full year, changed my lifestyle quite a bit. I rented a house near the theater.

A Broadway show is quite a feat to pull off. Having never had the experience before, I was intrigued with how everything worked. The cast was huge by Broadway standards.

Some of them were familiar faces, but most were new. I ended up being a "swing", which meant I was an extra person who studied everyone's show. In case of sickness, vacation, or accident, I would jump into their position to "take over" their spot for the evening.

10

VERONICA

Once we had decided upon the vehicle, the notion of connection was of importance. The vibration was in perfect harmony with our own. There was an openness available that was non-existent in others we observed.

Deciding to embark upon the endeavor, we reached our energy outward to introduce ourselves.

It was not an immediate connection, for there were others in the grouping who were endeavoring to connect themselves. It was of interest to us that of the individuals, one we could connect to, the best [April Crawford], was simply not interested.

The energy was of perfect harmony, however, not desiring to be intrusive, we waited.

Since time for us was not a factor, we hovered at a distance until the woman April would be able to connect.

Her laugh was infectious. We found ourselves feeling the sensation of her energy like a wave. The others would open the door, but she did nothing. Quite a difference that at first gave us much to ponder.

Different energies would arrive to blend with the others, but often the connection was faulty or just non-existent.

It was an evening of many stars that she opened the internal door. We know she did not really understand the opportunity that was upon us both.

We reached out, filling her form, while she moved out. It was a lovely exchange as we settled into her form.

Concerned for the April, we were mindful of her energy. She walked into a flowered glen, laying herself down to sleep under a lush willow. We know the time was now, so we began.

11

VERONICA

We recall with great clarity the relationship with the human experience. A desire above all else to expand our awareness deepened the projection of our essence into solid.

Not prepared for the thickness, we lived within a perceived enclosed consciousness for the first experiences.

Our higher awareness encouraged perseverance into the experience until we created a path of evolution.

Expanding the goal, while settling into the dramatic settings, each one more interesting than the last, we found need for advancement.

The physical condition brought forth much perception in the ways of our energy. Interaction from our cadre created deep attachments with others like ourselves. It was common ground we all stood upon... our unawareness bonding us all unconditionally in love.

It was blissful.

It was devastating.

It was an opportunity to become more that we were, so we engaged it.

Each engagement became more complicated than the last, until the lesson was complete.

We remember it all. Each nuance dances within us to this moment and beyond. We recall worrying about annihilation. We worried of becoming less than a footnote in the history of a world ever expanding. We were certain that we would never encounter our lovers again. We fixated upon the negative, often until we fell into a positive experience that changed our minds.

Thousands of moments live within us, even now. All that we have loved remains within us. There is still connection, laughter and tears. <u>All</u> remains a vivid experience to be treasured and continued.

We tell you this because we have been in your place, concerned about eternity and the next moments. We return now to give counsel so that you can walk through your lives with assurance.

Belief in who we are is unnecessary. Because we believe in you.

12

VERONICA

Having moved through the space as simple energy, we remained aware of the availability of complex ties... our evolution opening our consciousness to the desire of a participant of linear once again.

Not the habitat of a form to call our own, but a collaboration from one who would be aligned with us. Seeking this form, we moved through the abyss of awareness until we found what we looked for, a match energetically that transcended the usual decision to incarnate. The concept of retaining all of our experience so that we could participate in service was appealing. Would there be agreement?

We did not know...

However, we extended ourselves to the woman, for that was what she was, to align.

It was comfortable to reside in the form.   Her consciousness met us and moved aside to accommodate our energy.   The blend was appealing to both core energies.   We did have concern for her linear consciousness, but proceeded carefully so not to disturb her energy in the process.

In a breath, we arrived surprised by the fluidness of the connection, but even more surprise by those we encountered upon opening her eyes.

13

Pam
(April's View)

It was a time in my life where the feeling of belonging was becoming more important to me. My friend Pam was different than any of the other girls I found in the dance community. She was a seeker, looking for a spiritual connection that I had never considered.

Her travels had taken her through Buddhism, mediumship, and other esoteric thoughts, long before we met. In the long hours we spent together at the theater, I learned quite a bit about her and the spiritual road she traveled.

It was at the end of the run that her interest in channeling grew. I had never heard of it. The idea that someone would let a spirit talk through them was extremely foreign. Had I not known her so well, I might have though she was crazy.

Pam was sincere about everything and her desire to connect a huge one.

I listened politely, nodding my head at all the right intervals. She was my friend and I loved her. That was enough for me.

Michael

While in the show, I was dating a fellow named Michael. He was an Irishman. I used to call him a leprechaun, for indeed he was the embodiment of one.

We had met on a movie a few years before. I had fallen in love with his humor and heart. It should have been a happily ever after, but it wasn't. Michael was a Vietnam vet with drug and alcohol problems he never could conquer. I had toughed it out for a long time, but came to realize that I could not stay in the relationship.

It was one of the hardest decisions I ever made. I thought it would be better with someone else.

I had a summer job working as a cocktail waitress in a club in Beverly Hills. It was somewhat of a joke between my friends and me.   There was complete aversion between myself and alcohol due to my experience with Michael. I needed the money, so there I was.

It was the first time I had ever waited tables.

14

VERONICA

We recognize the need for some to have a more scientific explanation of origin.

It resides within us, but it is not at the forefront of our experience.   The feelings around origin are perhaps more interesting for those embarking upon the path.   Even the use of language limits the emotions regarding this.

Our goal in this dissertation is to give you our personal progress as it relates to our conversation with the April Crawford and our choice to speak through her.

We continued to advance even in the immediate moment.... so many avenues of making choices, a great struggle often.

As we became more, the experience continued until there was a solid experience laced with thought and emotion.

There were thousands of enactments where upon our energy evolved. The beginnings simplistic as the dramas unfolded. Each lesson broadened our knowing.

Other energies intersected, creating an intricate tapestry from the humble beginning of our first ones. We began to recognize the others, having encountered them often.

A move into a physical form was easy at first. It was the survival in the dense reality that shook ourselves down to the core.

An endless parade of creation making it a vivid participation. Not all the "lives" went well. All of the lessons not completely assimilated. Fortunately, the ability to recreate and balance was within our grasp.

It appeared that repetitive action was expected. Others were apparently having the same difficulty, for we "saw" them again and again. It was a cycle, but necessary to fully engage each new level. We were not disappointed, merely encouraged by the opportunity to get it right.

That was important.

15

VERONICA

A point of light projects itself through the walls of probability. Vibrating with more velocity each experience until a though links itself to the point.

Many repeat the process becoming more experienced and connected. A chain of events until the thoughts connect together.

A chain of events braided will form an array of light points. Each one more intense than the other, until the threads create a consciousness. The action again repeated, the threads begin to weave into an origin of a tapestry. Once this process begins, conscious awareness of the experience begins to continue the weave.

The memory of our first moment aware of ourselves amongst the intertwined threads is a vivid one.

The process by this moment was a path we followed continuously. The desire within reflected into the beginnings of a physical experience.

The first ones were logical. The nonphysical seemingly more useful. Our ability to move through the experiences did become more fluid. However, the experience remained difficult.

The driving force for expansion becoming overwhelming, we looked about us to get our bearings.

Those who were like us hovered in the periphery. We knew them to be familiar representatives of our core.

Thoughts of their progress [those who were like us] occurred to us, but were dismissed as too complex thought-wise in the moment.

We continued.

Each drawing us toward something undefinable. That is until we reached the threshold. In that moment the fog would lift, enabling us to complete the journey.

We felt amusement that it became a journey. Each moment becoming more clear as we transformed from nothing to something.

16

VERONICA

There came a moment when there was no longer need to continue in the linear space. Our energy desired reconnection to the whole. The lives were important, and locked into our memory. Each nuance holding a voice, action, and embrace of love.

Being a participant now in higher vibration called to us. We responded following the energy to distant viewpoints and harmonies.

We received much from those experiences. Expanding while connected to the whole, a vibrant experience. We found ourselves embracing new energy way beyond the linear experience. It provoked thought on multiple levels. If this were a description of those moments, we would continue in more detail.

This is about our aligning with the April Crawford from our perspective. Thus we will leave this for another place and time.

We kept expanding beyond levels and perimeters. Blending then separating. Blending and defining. Focusing then blending again.

We reached a place of wonder, realizing that what was really needed was an ebb and flow. The energy had always flowed but a return of that flow was the next phase of our journey.

Reaching within, there was a knowing of moving back through to linear to speak of our journey. For along the way, we saw how the denseness of physical participation can often become muddled. No longer would we incarnate, perhaps a partner to participate with?

We had heard of others who "borrowed" a physical form, but the idea was farfetched as the connection had to be a match.

17

April

Our gatherings became frequent.   The social aspect of it became a lifeline for me.   There was always food, laughter, and of course the channeling.

I sat through that part with respect, finding it somewhat interesting.

Usually there were just the four of us.   Ryan, Allen, Pam, and myself. On occasion, a fifth person named Brock showed up.   He was a puppeteer for the movies and was always a welcomed guest.

All I really know was the sense of community I felt.   These people I believe were my first real friends.

A sense of connection filled the room each time we got together. A recap of our day, while revealing how we felt about life was enlightening in so many ways.

My friend Pam had met Allen and Ryan in a channeling class with a woman named Shawn Randall. They would practice each time we met.

I was not sure how I felt about it all, but the community it created I treasured.

I would sit quietly curled up on the couch while they let go and let others come in. If I remember correctly, Ryan channeled an energy called "Hank", and Pam an energy called "Rasha". Allen, our resident thinker, struggled a bit to find the energy exchange with his.

One night I felt like I closed my eyes briefly. It had been a long day at the job and my whole body felt tired. Normally a quick cat nap refreshed me. Often I just closed my eyes, still listening to whatever was being said.

This night, however, I did not hear anything.

I slipped into a dream where I was dancing in a field full of radiant sunshine. It was warm, peaceful, and comforting.

Suddenly, I felt a sense of being watched. My eyes fluttered open to find myself the center of attention.

Pam, Ryan, and Allen were all staring at me with wide eyes.

18

April

"Are you okay?"

Pam seemed genuinely worried.   Both of the others in the group were quiet, but I could see the concern on their faces.

"Of course I'm okay," I replied.

"I just dozed off."

Allen then leaned forward and said, "Um, there was someone else here.   You do realize that don't you?"

I tried to look confident while searching fanatically in my mind for what had actually happened.   My whole life had been spent in control of myself.   I never partied, had never even taken a drink of alcohol until I was twenty five.

What had happened?

All three of them looked at each other trying to come up with a gentle way, I suppose, to tell me I had just been channeling.

My first reaction was "No I don't think so."

The three of them were pursuing this.

I was just along for the ride. Basking in all the energy was all I was really after. I wasn't even sure I believed in all the stuff. It was all interesting, but me?

Channeling?

Oh no!

Not me!

19

April

I spent the rest of the evening trying to piece together what had transpired.

A feeling of embarrassment filled me as I sat listening to my friends talking about this spirit that had come to talk to them. They said a name wasn't given but that it appeared to be a female.

Everyone agreed that she was quite the character and had been a lot of fun.

Sliding down into the chair I felt very left out. It was also very disconcerting to know my body had participated but I had not.

Pam asked where I had gone during the time. Actually, I couldn't remember. I thought that maybe I had fallen asleep.

Was I sleepwalking?

Sleep sitting?

Sleep talking?

I just didn't know.

Of course, Pam, Allen and Ryan thought it was great. All three of them were in a channeling class trying to accomplish what I apparently just did sitting on the sofa. They were over joyed. I was not sure how I felt.

The meetings, however, continued.

These three people eased me through my break-up. Their love and caring was addictive. So I found myself showing up just for "hugs". Aside from that, one incident, the channeling, remained the focus of the other three. I was there for the chips, soda and company.

It wasn't until a month or so later that they were visited by my Entity (at least that was the technical name.

Again, the entry was subtle.   Again, I was unaware until it was over, and yet again according to reports, it was amazing.

20

April

Every week we all looked forward to our meetings. There was a warm loving energy that melted away any stress of the day. Allen, Ryan, Pam, and I grew closer each time.

The evenings would start with Ryan and Pam practicing their channeling. They were taking channeling classes so the techniques they were learning helped them with their process.

I could curl up on the couch basking in all the energy. I was never interested in the channeling process, but the love I felt helped me in my own healing process.

The idea that I could channel did not really resonate with me. I felt uncomfortable not knowing what was going on. The others mentioned that they were semi aware of themselves during the process, so why couldn't I be?

It was upsetting not being able to know what was transpiring.   If I could have some knowledge, I thought I might feel better about it.

And for crying out loud!   They were all taking classes!   I was actually just a member of the peanut gallery.

Why was this happening to me, and not one of them?

Although all this was running through me, I still would not have missed a session.   Something was happening here that was blessed.   It was changing forever my view of the world and myself.

21

April

If I had not had the support of my friends, I would have felt like I was going crazy. Their embracement of what was happening to me gave me the courage to keep doing it.

Allen (who later became my husband) sought to record each session so that I could listen to it afterward. He was disappointed when I refused.

My voice was different. The idea of being a channel was not on my "to do" list. By not hearing it I was able to dismiss the whole experience.

Ryan was loving it while talking to this spirit, saying that he/she had a great sense of humor. A lot of wisdom was mixed into it as well (or so I was told).

Pam was a channel herself. In the classes she took, which all three were involved in, she was the star student. I would listen to her channel with great respect. The first spirit she brought through was Rasha. That energy slowly evolved into Hawthorne.

He was a great soul that had a lot of medical knowledge. It was always interesting to listen to him speak.

If my channeling was of that caliber, then I was okay. However, what I really wanted was to be more conscious. I guess I just wanted to know that I wasn't dancing on the table tops when I gave up my body.

Each time we met, which ended up being three or four times a week, I asked to be able to listen in.

22

April

There was a particular evening when we all decide to go out for dinner at our favorite Thai Restaurant. This time it was only Allen, Pam, and myself.

The restaurant, which was called the Chao Prya, had been a favorite of mine for years. I had introduced Pam to it during our dancing days. Allen and Ryan came along a few times, which converted them to faithful customers as well.

It was a wonderful evening with great food and friends. During the meal, we talked about life while including conversations about channeling in general. I was actually glad that we were doing something different. There was a need in me to get away for the whole process.

We finished early, but lingered to chat. I recall rubbing my eyes for they suddenly began to itch. I closed both of them only to reopen them with Pam and Allen staring at me wide eyed.

"What?" Why were they looking at me like that?

23

April

In the early days I was drawn to allow this energy to come in. The good feelings during and afterward were always welcome to me. If there were any hesitaitons, it was my lack of recall, and the often sudden onset of the channeling.

It did not scare me, but having full control of myself for most of my life, it made me uneasy.

If it had not been for my friends, Allen, Ryan, and Pam, I might have abandoned the whole process.

So, on this particular one evening when Allen, Pam, and I decided to have an outing to a local Thai restaurant in Hollywood, I remember sitting down and the next thing I knew we were leaving.

Somewhere in there was a meal that I missed. My friends shrugged it off as "VERONICA showed up".

What?

VERONICA did not eat (and never has) but she kind of cheated me out of a favorite meal. I was not pleased.

After that, I decided to have a conversation with her about her often abrupt entries.

24

VERONICA

It is said that all energy continues evolution unto infinity. Of this we concur, while still being able to embrace all of our participations.

Upon having moved through all the physical expectations of reincarnation, we found ourselves gliding effortlessly through space, seeking a connection to be of service to those still on the path.

We use the term "path", as it describes progress. It is important to be focused upon one's progress even after all the physical is said and done.

We were free to choose a vehicle to continue our service. The physical no longer adequate, while the concept of eternal brought no completion to our quest.

Thus, we searched for an energetic match to begin the service, which was the next stage of our development.

We sought circles of energy that had the commitment to spirit. Many were perceived and yet discarded.   The hope for communion almost despaired of.... until we felt the energy.

It was a small beacon of light amidst a circle full of seekers.   Though this energy did not seek the attractions to its vibration, it could not be dismissed.

25

VERONICA

The feeling of oneness beckoned us to the circle. Within it we could identify three of whom were extending themselves to the open field of vibration. The fourth one sat apart from the others, seemingly in observation.

We found this a curious contrast to the others. Of all the vibration being extended, it was this one that felt complete and compatible.

We engaged the circle, seeking more knowledge. What was the purpose?

26

VERONICA

As we moved from physical incarnation to participate in more advanced vibrations, we were compelled to remember the experiences. Knowing the difficulties associated with physical reality, we became interested in the ability to be of assistance.

Reality is rather like a stack of pennies, all taking up the same space with varied denseness. When one dismisses the continuance of linear physical, there is opportunity to move within the dimensions for more vibrational movement.

Having experienced these spaces, we became aware of the probabilities of being able to speak to those still in physical. In our search for opportunity of service, we realized that such a thing was actually available.

27

VERONICA

The love flowing from her heart was beautiful. We knew at once that this encounter would bring more light to an environment in danger of becoming darker.

We received an embrace from the energy collective, which helped us to decide upon the introduction. Whispering our vibration, we opened the door between us.

Her soul was surprised, but receptive. Her consciousness denied it was real. Her heart knew the value of the partnership. The blend, so complete, she passed us on her way to the universe, simply embracing the opportunity.

We felt relieved that the process was so smooth. It had been ever so long since ourselves felt the shape of a solid form.

We did not intrude upon the channel's psyche. We blended as smoothly as we could so not to cause any discomfort.   Sitting with her we found a multitude of connections.   There were no previous interactions in the physical, however, her energy matched our vibration perfectly.

For a great length of physical time, we sat within her energy field.   The gatherings were focused upon connecting to those like ourselves.   Therefore, we felt welcomed.

The others had their own path to follow with guides and energies matching their particular signature.   They were not aligned with us, we had found a place to sit so to speak, so we did.

What were the parameters of what they were seeking?   And finally, why was the quiet one so intriguing, yet not as available as the others?

At closer inspection we felt the presence of others similar to ourselves seeking connection with the other three. It was of interest to observe, so we did.

A flurry of energy from the three, while we still observed the fourth. A female, withdrawn, but present. The others pursuing, she was not. Our thoughts extended to her, but were not reciprocated in the way we hoped. Perhaps she was just unaware.

Each gathering we arrived, silent while waiting..... waiting to be received.

The others were exchanging, however, we still waited...

We observed her motion, finding it comforting and a good match.

Should we endeavor to introduce ourselves? A hesitation enveloped us while considering.

The channel's current name was April. An interesting word we had heard once in a life experience. At that time it was "Aperire", which was defined as "open".

28

VERONCA

With the arrival of finer energy, there was a desire to reach towards the physical denseness to communicate. We were advised that this type of connection would bring about an ability to assist those like ourselves who were still struggling through the process.

We had experience in how distorted and confusing linear reality could be. Assistance from spirit had benefitted our journey, thus we were compelled to render our energy to assist.

Knowing the energy needed to be compatible was our primary focus. A good match necessary for the process to unfold, we searched many places to find the connection.

Moving our energy through the reality, we noticed a small spark of light. Had we not looked closer, we may have dismissed it out of hand, however, as we approached, the spark grew larger until we could feel its vibration.

Surely this was what we sought.

We moved closer to feel the nuances of the energy. It appeared to be in the midst of a group of spiritualists attempting to connect to eternal.

What a great opportunity to connect with physical energy already seeking connection!

We felt the room, it felt inviting, however, upon closer inspection, the one true connection appeared completely uninterested in the blend. Curious. Curious that one so compatible would be not interested. The other three reaching outward towards us, but not a match. The true one relaxed, but disconnected.

We watched for much measured time, approaching at each opportunity. There was never an extension, but there was great openness. We rejoiced to have found her.

The challenge was integrating without direct permission. We acknowledged higher perspective that declared the moment should not be abandoned. So we continued to wait for the openness to continue.

We found her lovely.

29

VERONICA

It felt appropriate to hear her name, as it resonated with her openness to our energy. She was of great interest on many levels. A random occurrence that often permeates the physical energy. We had not notated its arrival before. We were, however, pleased to have initiated this relationship.

Realizing we perhaps had acted precipitously due to our great excitement, we slowed our vibration down to accommodate her.

It is not the nature of our spirit to force the issue. We would wait eternally if necessary to establish the relationship. We wondered as to why we had not encountered this woman before. Then again, we had not set forth to be of service in this way until these times. Our movement to embrace the dilemmas of others bringing a heart that has been enduring.

30

VERONICA

If one is to think in a linear way, all that would be relevant is the physical life.

We recall the experiences, all of them vividly. Each life an opportunity to advance and expand our energy. Most would say, especially in the linear, "To what end?"

You see that is the point, there is no end.

All consciousness exists eternally, seeking connection, expansion, and clarity.

Though it may sound daunting, It is not. It is merely a series of experiences remembered. The remembrance being relevant to more than the individual.

We have traveled throughout the linear and the eternal extensively. It's all relevant to us as it should be to you.

Once we reached a perspective of completeness, we began the search for opportunity to help others like ourselves to reach enlightenment. We were not dictated to... we decided internally to pursue opportunities to continue communication with linear participants.

Throughout our progression, we had the comfort of guides to ease the burden the physical brings with it. Not having this available would have made the journey more difficult with the experience harsher than it need to be.

We recall terrible moments of emptiness when it seemed the reality was impossible to endure. We have endured in spite of ourselves and the choices made. We attribute this success to those who were of different perspective, those whose view was truth rather than contrived manmade nonsense.

Thus we begin here.... and acceptance of responsibility to reach beyond parameters to assist those seeking truth. We have a clear view now and wish to share it.

It cannot be said more plainly.

31

VERONICA

There will be a moment when all of you will arrive to the conclusion that one must continue to thread.

A thread is defined by those who would lead others who may be just behind you on the path.

A thread can be an actual lifeline to those becoming wary of fending for themselves.

So we arrived to find our viewpoint would have value. A refusal to be helpful was simply not an action we could choose. So we were pleased after searching, to find a suitable partner for the endeavor.

The woman seemed oblivious at first to our tappings, but persistence is an appreciation we acquired over the lifetimes.

We realized with pause that she had the choice to reject our suggestion to merge.

Therefore, we tread softy, attempting to extend comfort. Her reactions, had the situation been not so serious, would have been amusing.

We wondered at why such a great match was provided by one who had not lived so spiritually, nor had sought us.   Assured by the ability to move through her, we gained patience.   Opposition was not the difficulty. it was actually the ease by which the whole process was occurring.

We were pleased.... she not so much.

32

VERONICA

There were many starts and stops as the relationship progressed.   All in all, nothing but expansiveness came from the union.   There are few antidotes without a bit of magic attached to them, as all were magnificent from our viewpoint.

Once the April Crawford was comfortable, the rest was a smooth sail into eternal bliss. We find the opportunity enchanting as it was the moment we connected. We find it that way still.

Spirit is always appreciative when those encumbered by bodies are able to participate without fear.

Fearless is a word we would use to describe this channel.   That trait has only grown over the perceived linear timeline. For that we are grateful.

33

VERONICA

We beseech all to embrace their connection with spirit. The linear reality is a volatile environment.

Those who endeavor to traverse its corridors can use all the connection they can create.

Those in our realm are ready to assist. No agendas, timeframes, or dramatic events to blur the ebb and flow of energy that is available.

Take time to embrace those in non-physical who love you.

Spiritual perspective often can be a life vest in the sea of confusion.

We   cherish   the   connection.

34

APRIL

The summer progressed while the four of us continued our sessions. It had risen often beyond the original four sessions per week, often.

Allen, who lived the farthest away (about an hour) I thought struggled the most. He worked fulltime as well. The sessions would last sometimes well after midnight.

I believe Ryan worked a fulltime job too, however, he lived just "over the hill" from Pam's apartment. His drive could not have been more than half an hour or less.

I was renting a house in Century City that was about a 15 minute drive. At midnight though, it could seem endless.

In retrospect, I do not know how Allen did it. Surprisingly, he was the most gung-ho about the meetings. He was also the person who recorded the sessions faithfully.

Pam was (and is) the eternal seeker. When I met her she was always experimenting with religion and psychic things. We spent many many hours in the bowels of the Shubert theater discussing spirituality. I should say it was more of a lecture type of situation, as my experience was limited to Catholicism.

Pam had explored Buddhism and other paths to enlightenment, while I had made my departure from religion.

A common joke amongst all my childhood friends was that we had banked enough masses during our parochial school years to give us credit served well into our nineties. It had been years since graduation, and equally as long since I stepped inside a church.

Pam had not been a Catholic, but knew about a lot of its practices. She desired to be connected her whole life. I had taken a lot for granted, being more interested in living a very physical life.

We were an odd match, but the friendship became solid.

35

APRIL

As we explored our abilities, both Pam and I found that we were a pretty good match. When I would sail out too far, Pam would be able to come retrieve me. There seemed to be a lot of support that we were becoming aware of.

We all had started meeting once a week at Pam's apartment. Before we knew it, the meetings had expanded to three or four nights a week. Of course it was a social event, but it was becoming peaked with interest for what was afoot.

Allen, the information saver, always brought his recorder. I thought it was unnecessary, but he was adamant about the importance. (We still have all the cassette tapes.)

We would start the evenings with a little food. We all were becoming fast friends so all of us were interested in the others' lives.

About an hour into the evening, we would all settle down to begin the channeling.

If I remember correctly, Ryan would begin with an energy we all called "Hank".

36

April

I remember feeling so awkward returning back to my body after sessions. Going so far out, I did not have recall of what transpired, nor of the time.

Ryan, Allen, and Pam had had an evening of adventure, while I was left ignorant of what transpired.

At first it was difficult to be enthusiastic about the information, because there was absolutely no memory.

I can remember conversation with Allen, where he was jumping out of his skin with joy at the contact. I was less than enthused. In fact, there was even thought of, "No. I do not want this".

Allen of course was incredulous that I would even consider stopping.

During the sessions, which were now numbering at least four times a week, all of them asked the energy if they could allow me to be more present. That in doing so, perhaps I could become more comfortable with the sessions.

To my friends, this was imperative. But could it be done?

No one was sure, but they all assured me that they would ask.

Having good friends is a wonder.   They all persisted until they achieved an agreement.

37

April

The first time I was aware of another voice, I was a bit taken back. Thoughts moved through me but I did not generate them. My throat and vocal chords were engaged, but it was like they were in remote control.

There were the same feelings that were present in the other sessions, only I was not off in a dream state. I was aware of the energy moving through me and felt the words form, but it wasn't me saying them.

Thankfulness waived through me, for my eyes were closed. I did not have to watch my friends talking with my body, but not me. It was all unsettling, but at least now I could hear what was occurring.

This energy used different parts of my vocal chords, so there was a bit of a strain upon them as the words came out. Interesting, since I never had felt residual fatigue in them when returning from sessions before, when I was unaware [of what was being said].

38

April

The words of another echoed through my thoughts. It surprised me that I could still think while it occurred. Instead of being uncomfortable, I found that the love actually soothed me.

Far from being what I had envisioned, the words spoken impacted me greatly.

Allen had told me that they had named the energy VERONICA and that she was something to behold. Naturally, without me being there, I was skeptical.

This first meeting was extremely special, for at last I felt "introduced" to VERONICA. She was quite funny and wise. All of my discomfort left me. I knew I could trust her and that what was coming out of my mouth was good and helpful.

In later times, I would "sense" her passing me on her way in. It was always a warm moment as we embraced spiritually.

39

April

Being able to hear what was going on offered other benefits as well. The "feeling" of the energy made me fell terrific.

Being around little kids when I taught dance made me susceptible to all kinds of ailments. Sore throats were a common occurrence, accompanied by a loss of my voice. I also would get a nagging cough that would linger on long after the cold was gone.

Over my life I learned to expect the debacle and just dealt with it.

The first time we were in a session where I almost did not show up because my voice was nonexistent, the energy (soon to be called VERONICA) would somehow dispose of the laryngitis. By the end of the evening, most symptoms would be greatly diminished or gone.   It was rather astounding.

40

VERONICA

Having valued the experiences of physical, there was much desire to be something more. Would there be an opportunity to engage those who had lost their way?

How fortunate to be cognizant of the workings of one's own evolution. The lives, not effortless in their enactments, should be gleaned for others to evolve. It was a question we posed to all of our awareness as the time to cease incarnations became closer.

To receive all the workings of the perceived evolutions, it became apparent that the next phase was one of nonphysical awareness.

It came upon us swiftly this feeling of wishing to connect. At first it was not readily available. Much ado being made by energy around us. Soon it was obvious, this path to be taken.

Would it be better to guide or leave it to the energy to find its way? We felt deeply the pull towards the first choice.

There had been moments in our own process where the vision of spirit guided through many a dark moment. It felt appropriate to now do the same.

So it is.

It was a feeling of knowing when we reached out for a vessel. Past relationships set aside as we searched for the perfect match.

If there had been a time reference, we would respond that it was long.

Female, but oddly removed from all of our experiences. How could this be? To arrive at a match not previously experienced? Our energy quickened with anticipation.

We reached out.

Her name, April, resounded within.

There was no fear from the form, so we ventured forward.

No intentions other than to speak through the body. Warm response. Warm giving of our core. It was indeed a perfect match. What was left was to work out the specifics so that the April would continue.

41

April

So with the support of my friends, I continued the channeling even though I did not remember a thing afterward.

It was like a deep sleep with no dreaming. My body relaxed so much that the only true memory of the sessions was a feeling of flotation.

Everyone was always in awe and amazed with this energy they named "VERONICA". Since I had no memory, I had to go with what they told me.

We must have been crazy in those days. We were all trying to make a living, but would end up meeting three times a week with the sessions lasting till well after midnight. Now, this was not so bad for Ryan, Pam and I, but Allen lived a <u>full</u> hour away and had a full time job. He had to be getting home well after one AM and I knew he had to be at work by nine AM each week day.

Allen, of course, would say it was well worth it to him.   The rest of us lived minutes from Pam's apartment and we had more flexible schedules.   It must have been difficult for him.   I would say though, that he was the most dedicated of all of us.

42

April

I did become comfortable channeling in our little group. We would begin the evening with a little food and drink. It was like meeting up with family for dinner. In a big place like Los Angeles, that in itself was worth showing up for.

Each one of us would take turns providing the "meal" for the evening. At the time, I was a huge lover of Thai food. When it was my turn to provide, I naturally ran to my favorite restaurant to get all of my favorite dishes. Pam was already a convert, but I wasn't sure about Allen and Ryan.

Ryan was a laid back fellow who was pretty amiable about everything. Allen was more of an enigma. He was quiet and very serious about all the channeling. When I brought the Thai food into the apartment, I could see by his face he wasn't pleased.

I handed him a Thai iced tea and could almost predict that he would hate it.

He opened the container and managed a slight smile. I could tell he felt obligated to drink some to be polite. He closed his eyes and took a sip. The look of utter shock on his face remains vivid in my mind twenty years later.

Eyes wide, he continued to sip, claiming it was fantastic. At the time, I was not sure if he was telling the truth. However, he still orders it to this day.

43

April

Our group became a "rock" for me over time. It was an age of growth for all of us. As I have said, we met as often as we could. Every session was exciting and interesting.

Pam continued to bring through an energy called "Rascha". It helped me feel better about my own channeling because the sessions were always solid and uplifting.

Ryan always brought in Hank, who was not so informative, but certainly entertaining.

For a long time I was unconscious for any channeling of VERONICA. I guess I should describe (at least what was told to me) some of the first interactions with her.

Allen has always told me that when VERONICA first came through, it was with such great force that for a moment they were all taken aback. Most energy that came through was a little softer spoken.

Allen said he led the initial interview, because he found it intriguing that this energy was so different [different than the others that come through April and the others before VERONICA came through: A note by Allen].

I think it was Allen that ended up calling her VERONICA. [Actually, it was Ryan who came up with that name. *Another note by Allen*].

I can remember coming out of trance with all three of my friends rejoicing that she agree to the name.

I felt slightly left out, but somehow knew all of this was important. Little did we all know that someday VERONICA would be well known.

I would have shuddered at the time to go public with my channeling. I was comfortable in our little cocoon and planned on staying there.

44

April

The summer of 1989 truly brought about a maturing from me. Our group met at least three times a week. Allen, Ryan, Pam, and I felt like family. It was a mass therapy session for all of us.

Pam was a movie stand-in, so she was always putting in very long days. Ryan was a business guy and Allen was an executive for a computer company.

I was still dancing, but I had also extended into being a spokes model. It was steady money, but it required trips out of town.

By Fall, the "season" had started and I found myself on the road a lot. Our group remained number one on my agenda. Often I would arrive straight from the airport for our sessions.

All of us were busy, but made the time to be there, even if it meant a lack of sleep.   I felt energized.

The channeling refreshed me in a great way.

If I felt tired or even under the weather, after a channeling, whatever ailed me disappeared almost completely.

We would all joke about that it was really a tune up session not a channeling one.

It was such a comfortable fit that I never wanted it to end.   It was life changing and positive.   Much more than I ever could have imagined.

45

April

It was during all the sessions that Allen and I became closer. He lived an hour away from the sessions and worked a fulltime job. We would often meet at 7 PM without ending sometimes until well past midnight.

I really don't know how he did it, having made the trip out to Moorpark often since then. It's a tedious drive on the best of days. He says that he often felt "out of body" by the time he arrived home. He must have been a zombie at work the next morning.

We often joke about it now. Good thing we were all young at the time. The thought of that trip makes us both tired just thinking about it.

With all the time we spent together, I had never been alone with Allen. The other two were always included.   So it felt a bit awkward when Allen invited Pam and I to separate concerts. I was invited to see The Who at the Coliseum in Los Angeles.

I remember feeling nervous when Allen arrived to pick me up.   There had always been buffers between us to keep the conversation going.   This was the first time with just the two of us.

46

April

I supposed I talked way too fast while really saying nothing.   Looking back I still felt embarrassed.

It was because I was so used to the others being around that I acted so stupid.

Allen came to my house to pick me up way early. I can remember wondering how I could keep the conversation going.   For some reason I felt awkward.

As the night proceeded, I found myself becoming more comfortable. His brothers and sister were also at the concert, and I go introduced when we got there.

I had not seen them in concert before. It was spectacular in a lot of ways.

I had been bringing forth an energy in our channeling sessions named Lizette. She was dreaming while she came to visit from 17th century France. I could feel her very close and though she might get a thrill out of the experience. (I will go into more detail of Lizette in another chapter.)

I told Allen that I was letting Lizette come in. He was pleased to be able to facilitate the experience.

The audience was chanting "Who, Who, Who" when Lizette arrived. Allen was holding onto my waist so that Lizette would feel more secure. She thought that this was our King, for it reminded her of her own time, when the King would step forward out on the balcony in Versailles.

She also thought the crowd was booing the king. Allen told her what was occurring.

He said that they were not booing, they were saying "Who! Who! Who!" And she understood.

I could feel her appreciating the concert, although a lot of it she did not understand.

It was cool for me just to be able to allow her to have the experience.

I stepped back into my form and enjoyed the rest of the concert. Allen and I had passed the awkwardness. We both (or at least I did) felt more comfortable being alone. An expansion had occurred. At the time I didn't think much of it. We simply had had a nice time. I felt so comfortable that I invited him in after we got back to my house.

There was nothing on my mind except I was enjoying his company. Allen, on the other hand, politely declined my invite. I was not offended because I knew he had a long drive home ahead of him.

He hugged me and quickly left. It was only much later that he revealed that he had kicked himself all the way home.

47

April

Lizette (since she was really a visitor from another time who was dreaming) was fascinated. She actually thought that one of the people on stage must be our King. Her only experience with this type of crowd was at Versailles with Louis XVI.

I only heard about this after the fact. To let Lizette fully in, I of course had to be fully out. There was a fondness that grew between us since we passed each other in the exchange. I felt happy that she was able to experience something out of her time.

Lizette had let me experience her surroundings as well. I found myself in a rather comfortable bedroom. On "awakening", the first thing I noticed was the smell.

A rather farm smell that was pungent.

Lizette had satin sheets upon a rather small bed that faced out towards paneled windows that went floor to ceiling.   There were brass latches that if opened, would allow the windows to open.   I only knew this because some of them were.

I was rather taken back by the realness of my surroundings.   I could hear sheep bleating and a distant rooster.

48

April

So the summer dragged on. Well, I suppose "drag" is the wrong term to define it. There was an endless time of sessions, each one becoming more interesting than the next.

All of us grew closer, however, Allen and I were forming a bond that simply could not be touched by the others. Of course I was oblivious to most of it.

I knew I felt close to Allen, but I was also in a pattern of dating inappropriate men. Allen must have been driven mad by my refusal to see the truth. Somehow, I kept making excuses for the feelings.

On the other hand, it worked out pretty well for the both of us in the end.

It was well into the fall of the year 1989. Our group had established a great rhythm.

As I've said, we were meeting several times a week. One night a two dimensional being came through both Pam and me while channeling for the group. We were all sitting on the couch and Allen was feeling energy by lifting his hand up. I matched his movements, finding a deep connection with him that I never felt before.

We were sitting on either side of our friend Pam on the couch. The two dimensional being in the middle of its own experience caught Allen and I up in its vibration. Allen's eyes were upon me as we connected in the dual dimension. It was one of the most intimate experiences I had ever had up to that point.

It wasn't sexual at all, rather so spiritual that we both felt lifted out of our seats.

I remember trying to contain my laughter. It was so joyous that was all I felt like going... was laugh.

After that I realized something was going on that was beyond anything of my previous experiences.

I had always liked Allen, but after that night, things changed between us. I felt myself looking forward to his next visit.

The energy increased until one evening after a session at my house, Ryan and Pam had left. Allen and I were getting for him to leave until I realized that I did not want him to.

As we went for the door, I reminded him that he had wanted a copy of a CD I had called the "Fairy Ring".

I said, "OK, we still have to copy that for you".

Allen, being his polite self, said, "Well, maybe next time."

I replied with, "Why not copy it now?"

Before he could comment, I had set up the tape to be copied.

He sat back down on the couch, and I felt comfortable and happy that he stayed.

49

April

With a great deal of clumsiness I managed to insert a blank tape into my stereo to copy the Fairy Ring.

In retrospect, I felt like I appeared foolish and desperate. In the moment, Allen had settled back on the couch and for the moment, appeared comfortable to be there.

I was in agony trying to define why I had suggested he stay for a copy of the Fairy Ring. The evening was complete. Pam had long since left. There was no reason for Allen to still be there. Oh yes, the tape. However, that could have been done at any time.

Did I look manipulative?

Was I manipulative?

Did he think I was manipulative?

All these questions raced through me as I sat quietly next to Allen on the coach.   All of my bravado was fading.   All I really knew was that I did not want Allen to leave.

What did that mean?

I did not know.

I was elated he accepted.   I would have to wait to see what transpired.

50

April

The Fairy Ring CD was magical. I had always loved it from the first time I heard it. That night I put the blank cassette in so that I could copy it. Normally, I would have put it in speed record, but for some reason I let it play, while Allen and I sat nervously on the couch. I thought for sure he would question why I was doing it the way I was.

The realization that I even suggested he stay after everyone had left just to record some music made me feel like he could see right through me. I wasn't even sure why I did it, so I hoped he would not question the situation.

Fortunately, he just sat back and listened to the music.

51

April

So Allen and I ended up talking for hours that evening. The feeling between us was one of warmth and love. I don't think either of us was expecting to start a relationship, but that's what happened.

In life he was a solid guy who had trouble being vulnerable, but went the extra distance to let me know he cared.

In channeling, he was my rock. With his presence I felt invincible and could explore the process because I knew he was there to protect and help me.

There was also great encouragement. I started channeling in 1989. It took until 1999 for Allen to be able to talk me into doing the channeling work publicly and as a business.

I did not want to share with those who may have judged me. In this life I learned I had a goal of acceptance, which made perfect sense as I reviewed my early life. Channeling did not fit comfortably into my life, so I wanted to keep it apart from who I thought I was.

It took more than ten years before I would channel for anyone outside of my familiar circle. Allen, who in 1991 became my husband, was always encouraging me to allow others to experience VERONICA. I knew it was something I should do, but always came up with an excuse not to.

Allen and I moved to Tarzana, California, renting a house that was just about equal distance to both our worlds. It was a beautiful venue to host channeling circles, which we did do often.

Pam and Ryan became busier with their lives and so it became mostly Allen and I.

Allen worked as an executive at a computer company called "Tandon" when I first met him. He had always wanted to be in entertainment and was thrilled when he was offered a job as Director of Business Affairs at Digital Domain.

I continued to teach dance, while channeling often.

It wasn't until much later when we had move to another house that I even entertained the idea of channeling for a living.

52

April

I grew up a good Catholic girl. All girl academy in high school, Catholic grade school. I was brought up with all the tradition. I felt a connection with religion while small. It wasn't until I was in high school that I began to question the truth of it.

The nuns were good women, albeit delusional in their perceptions of reality. They insisted upon total compliance with the rules. A lot of what went on in the academy was completely opposite of the rules.

I believe that my attraction was past life based. Somewhere I had been religious nun/brother/priest.

The appeal in this life was the connection to another time and place. The academy was built in the 1920's in a quaint Midwestern town. I felt connected to it almost irrationally. At the time, I would sit in the cloister absorbing the atmosphere. I felt like I wanted to jump into the 20's and be there. A loneliness for what had been was a vivid experience for me.

In those days I did not have the vocabulary to identify a past life experience. All I could do was imagine what it was like to be there earlier in the timeframe.

I can recall hearing voices and feeling sensations that if I had shared them, I probably would have been suspended.

My spiritual heart I kept to myself. I knew I did not want to be a nun, but felt the experience was in me somewhere.

It was the internal voice that sat with her arms folded during religion class. I remember questioning a regulation or concept and getting smacked down by the nun in charge.

In my senior year it became a sporting event to see how many questions I could ask before being sent out of the class.

I was not the most popular girl. I spent most of my free time in dance class, missing most typical high school events. Most would have described me as aloof, but I would have said, "No, I am shy."

What I did in dance was a contradiction, but I spent a lot of time in deep thought about reality. The voices encouraged that practice. So religion class did not always provide me with an "A". I asked too many questions.

One thing that did get a lot of attention was "Mass". In my 12 years of school, I figured I went to mass most every day. This, according to my belief, provided me with a free "get out of going to mass" card for at least ten years into my adulthood.

53

April

Of course life after high school did change. I was caught up in running my dance studio, going to college, and trying to break into show biz.

I lived at home, but really was never there. Between all the activities, I was rarely home. My religious moments were also few and far between. I had embraced my ten years hiatus from mass, only going to church on Christmas. My mom was always after me to go on Sunday, but it just didn't feel right.

The whole life in Michigan was beginning to feel tight. In the back of my head, I was already living in California. I knew it was the place for me to be. So I began saving money from all of my jobs. There needed to be at least ten thousand dollars available because I also needed to buy a car to take me there.

So for the next couple of years, I was hell bent on saving as much as I could.

There was a reprieve where I went to Miami to do a show for 6 months. It enabled me to save even more money. I knew where I had to be, and I did not slow down for anyone.

In the summer of 1979 I was ready. I packed my belongings and flew out to "Californ-i-e". I had purchased a used car in Michigan, but was told by my parents that they would prefer that my brother would be driving it out.

I appreciated that my parents were just being protective, having no problem with my brother driving it out.

So there I was, July 25, 1979, in a hotel room. My brother Cole had just flown back to Michigan. I was alone in a huge strange city, hoping to get work as a dancer.

Looking back, I marvel at my courage. A 23 year old kid who found an apartment and proceeded to make her way into the dance world.

54

April

During all these times I kept my spiritual side close to me. I did not engage anyone about their belief systems, however, in Los Angeles, I encountered quite an array of them.

While doing 42nd Street at the Schubert Theater in the early 1980's, I met Pam (who would later become part of our channeling group). She was certainly a seeker. She was constantly experimenting with a lot of different things.

Buddhism was one avenue that she was traveling that she invited me to attend. I cared about her a lot but the chanting simply did not resonate with me.

She was also the one who introduced me to the concept of channeling. At the time, I thought it was all nonsense. I listened to the stories about it with politeness, but never took it seriously. I guess the good Catholic girl still had a firm grip upon me.

55

April

I remember the first months of the channelings as a struggle to be a part of it.   I realized and appreciated what was occurring, but in essence felt extremely left out.

I did not feel or remember anything of the sessions, which led me to be uncomfortable.   Allen, Pam, and Ryan were always full of tales after the session.   All of them were positive.   I completely trusted all three of them, so I continued.

When the sessions began, I could feel a whoosh of air passing my face.   I always closed my eyes so when it occurred I saw nothing.   I began to have a sensation of floating, sometimes landing in places that appeared rather dreamlike.   It was not unpleasant, but I really wanted to experience and hear what everyone was raving about.

So with Allen's help, I put in a request to "hear" what was going on. I could sense the presence, but hearing was important to me.

The first time it all came together I almost recanted the wish. When the energy "whooshed" past me, I felt taken by the hand. I could hear a voice in my head, only it wasn't mine.

The normal thoughts of processing words and language was no longer mine to deliver. It was very strange. I knew it was my vocal cords. I could feel them vibrating, but it wasn't me at all. Very strange it was.

The voice was deeper. The foreign thoughts taxed my brain. But I could hear what was transpiring and it was good. This force who was dubbed VERONICA by the group did have a purpose for coming through me. I was surprised, but honored.

So I decided to continue. After a while I began to find the opportunity to "visit" other realms during the sessions, which I found more interesting.

Just knowing that I could listen gave comfort and the strength to continue.

56

April

I never sought the ability. I never ever thought my journey would lead me to this moment.

The first half of my life so physical with all the dancing, now replaced with this connection with spirit.

I still dance for recreation, but the majority of my day is spirit channeling and writing.

I feel blessed to have had this ability, perhaps all along. It just shows me how the twists and turns of life eventually lead you right where you are supposed to be.

VERONICA's energy heals me on many levels. One of them is when I may have picked up a bug and would not be feeling well.

While in trance, she realigns my energy in such a way that whatever was aching me, disappears.

I can't tell you how many viruses she has taken out of me. It's not so noticeable to those who see me only occasionally.

To Allen, it's amazing. He has seen me totally wiped out before a session, and completely better afterwards.

57

April

So it has been quite a journey. My trust in VERONICA is complete. I know that all that comes from her is real and heartfelt. The honor for being able to do this increases every day.

We now do groups occasionally but it is mostly phone sessions. I never listen to the information and am always amazed how well VERONICA is received. I always want everyone to have a great experience when they talk to VERONICA, so I stay as far out as I can.

In the beginning I was nervous, especially during some of the first sessions.

Allen had been on a metaphysical message board, and ran into a woman named Lisa. They conversed for a long time about channeling until one day she asked for a session.

Of course Allen was all excited and said yes immediately. I, on the other hand, felt nervous.

What did VERONICA know about talking on the phone?

How would it work?

Could she really read energy over the phone?

I was filled with a million questions, with great reservations.

Looking back I laugh because poor Allen had to literally walk me through it. I sat down at the table while Allen kept telling me it would be fine.

Really?

Well, VERONICA came through strong. I remember her asking Allen if she needed to hold the phone. He said, "No, it's a speaker phone."

After that, I did not remember anything until Allen said to me, "Well Babe, you made it through."

58

April

It was a huge step for me. I was elated and thankful that it went well. The beginning of a vocation that has now gone on for over ten years.

Allen laughs a lot when he relates that it took me ten years to get comfortable. Add that to the mix and I realize that while writing this I have been channeling over twenty years.

VERONICA reminds me often not to be too attached to time. It does not exist in other realities.

I guess if there was one thing I wanted everyone to understand, is that my relationship with VERONICA has developed into a great friendship.

Some have said that it's too scary to open yourself to spirit. Well I didn't try, it just happened.

I learned that spirit is completely loving.   The support I feel from her is the best.

59

VERONICA

The concept of eternal is always a bit daunting for those who participate in a linear life.   It is necessary to fully focus intently while living a life.

Our environment offers opportunity to focus upon many items at the same time.   There are no parameters or limits to what one wants to experience.

Imagine if you will, a more fluid tapestry that changes its texture merely by a directed thought.   It is an environment of flexibility that we live in now. Each level becoming more and more conducive to our energy.

The concept that when a physical life ends that that is the end of your evolution is inaccurate.   Each experience builds upon the preceding one, offering the energy the opportunity to advance a bit further.

It is not exhausting in the way some of you perceive it.

60

VERONICA

We, having moved through the linear evolution, found ourselves in the wake of eternal opportunity. Other realms also offered experience that allowed our energy to advance even further.

With all this talk of advancement, it is important to realize that the "knowing" must be shared with those who are perceived to be following.

Our path became filled with desire to lend a hand to those who struggled with their own journey.

In this new perspective, we were able to perceive the half-truths and fallacies that were being portrayed in the current linear.

We had been assisted on our journey so we set about to extend help to the present timeline moment.

The difficulty was observed in finding a vehicle to convey the information to those still in the thick environment of the earth plane.

We had known of others who were successful in obtaining a connection with an open linear being. We had considered it an easy attainable connection.

Our awareness increased with each new experience, so we were able to be cognizant of opportunity for uniting.

At first glance, we began reaching out for similarity of energy, which there seemed to be a bountiful supply.

Upon second glance, the frequency of energy was not always a suitable match to ours.

Conferring with others, we found that to be of service in the way we desired, the match had to be a complete one. All aspects needed to be in harmony to achieve the right ability to use the dense physical form.

Traversing the cosmos one finds many probabilities, but we were seeking the perfect match. Our purpose was to individually work with energies to help them through difficult dramas of physical. We knew full well that the uniqueness of each soul would need us to be integrated fully into a form.

This would enable us to recall the physical experience fluidly and be able to respond in language that an embodied soul would understand.

We found it was not to be so easy.

61

VERONICA

Our energy, having had a full experience within the linear, rose to various levels within what is called the eternal.

The ability to transcend experience, while becoming engaged with higher forms of our energy was indeed a magnificent progression.

It was fulfilling, enabling our consciousness to blend with others, until it sustained a higher perspective.

The beauty of this enables the singularity of the experience to remain, while combining with other levels of energy. The ultimate moment being one in total union with our source.

As stated, the search for a vehicle to participate through in the linear was not an easy endeavor.

Of course the anticipation of such a union was exciting.   Thus, the finding of it was a critical moment even in our own evolution.

As energy develops, the personal agenda is often complete, allowing energy like ourselves to evolve to a level where the advancement of others becomes the focus.

Thus it was for us.   As we blended with others, we realized the importance of the extension of our experience into those not as advanced on their own path.

Conferring with others became a great desire within as we opened the pathways from our own environment.

62

VERONICA

The decision to stop the incarnational process began as a deep thought evolving into a choice to extend ourselves to other levels.

This dissertation is not about our position in the other realms. It is about our choice to connect to make the path easier for those who trailed behind us. To measure it in years by linear is not relevant. If asked, the plane of existence, it is the Causal Plane. A blending of others like ourselves who have ascended to a different perspective.

There would be three thousand or so, who are part of the collective, while still experiencing the singular awareness.

All have history. All have experience. All are of the mind to be of service to those in the linear.

Thus we began our journey to see an avenue of availability. The ability to connect vibrationally while speaking through one who lives in the linear. Not such an easy task we were to learn.

63

VERONICA

We have been asked by those who wonder why we choose to speak through a woman at this time and place. There is always a question of "what we get out of it."

We smile to ourselves even now that the linear has not changed all that much since our incarnational cycle.

Our journey brought forth much evolvement with continuance in other realms thereafter. We now reside within a collective of energy possessing in the blend over 3,000 experiences of various levels of vibration.

We know that the definition of "level" is important in the timeline state. Indeed it does not remain so in the eternal.

It is vibratory placement that defines and resonates with all participants here.

64

VERONICA

There has always been a feeling of care for those still moving through their reincarnational cycle. Upon my own completion, the energy shift was of the utmost welcome. Moving through the energy of eternal was a bit easier from our perspective.

There has been observation continuously throughout. It has been considered a disconnect from the truth, from the viewpoint of eternal.

Thus, the inclination to get the message of ease to those physical. Our focus was upon finding the energetic match so that we could be lended the form.

65

VERONICA

We had arrived at the Causal Plane of existence after experiencing thousands of physical lives and Astral Plane experiences.

It is a vibration of energy that no longer requires manifestation. Linear words cannot describe it. The plane offers a memory of potential for all souls. Our place is to relay the information to the physical plane for those who seek.

The so-called past and future exists for all in this realm.

For our energy to fulfill its destiny, we (combined with other Entities) sought the physical counterpart to help deliver the messages to those who would seek.

Our hearts burst forth towards the opportunity. The remaining obstacle was to find a physical match. We thought it an easy task. It was not.

Seeking those incarnated who were also seeking the divine was plentiful. It was the perfect match that was narrow.

Our focus to find the one consumed our thoughts. Without the measurement of time it was difficult to connect with a reality that adhered to it so completely.

66

VERONICA

To achieve the connection, advice from higher realms included the deeper knowing of ourselves. The internal process possibly more accurate than the outward one.

It was understood that the physical realm was now filled with potential hosts for higher knowledge. We approached the moment with reverence. This connection would be a unique experience for both ourselves and them.

Slowing our vibration, we began to move through the solid space. So many incarnates that wished to participate.... alas, not the correct match.

67

VERONICA

Many would ask if we looked down from the heavens upon an earthly moment to connect. We would say that it was more of an internal search where we were able to see the availability energetically.

We recall the group of which the April Crawford sat with.   It appeared to be open with those participants available to possible partnership.

The April Crawford was there, but it appeared to be more of an observation for her than an openness. We passed over the others to see her more clearly.

Was this an opportunity?

We speculated upon a blend, deciding against such measures as her energy did not feel receptive. Pity. It held much promise.

We returned many times in anticipation of a change of venue. It was not until she had slipped into sleep one evening that we venture to extend ourselves fully.

It was successful.

68

VERONICA

Many in the linear would believe that this union might have been forced upon the April Crawford. On the contrary, it was merely an extension of ourselves to her.

Since it was not part of her perceived plan to channel our energy, it was up to us to extend the invitation to bring her along on an endeavor that could help many.

Nothing was forced.

The match so perfect, the mere intention of our energy to speak allowed us easy access to her form. Our encounter an easy one that left her feeling revived and invigorated.

Her conscious self of April had difficulty at first due to the extreme controlling nature she had over her linear self.   Anything outside of certain parameters was suspect.   Thus, we endured here perspective for a long linear time.   It was all worth the wait.

To us it was perfect.   For us we were able to perceive all the positive outcomes.   We were patient, and actually with the help of the Allen Crawford, so was she.

69

VERONICA

Our energies mingled for the first time while she had fallen asleep. It was an opportunity for jus to test the waters without mishap.

We had approached her several times. Her focus was extremely outward, so her ability to perceive our internal presence went undetected. It enabled us to verify with certainty the incredible match between us.

We were surprised and delighted. Fortunately for the situation, April was involved with those who desired and sought the connection of channeling spirit. Out of the four, April appeared totally disinterested in the process for herself. She was there for her friends and the beautiful energy that filled the room each time.

70

VERONICA

We continued our connection each time the group assembled.   It was a beautiful experience which eventually rose to the moment where we could speak.

The higher elements of the April responded well to our overtures.   The difficulty (as we knew it would be) was with the conscious self that had already begun to define itself, and channeling was not part of that definition.

Patience.

It would require patience.

Fortunately, we were abundant in the patience element.   This match was pure, and worth the effort to bring it into fruition.

71

VERONICA

We can recall our first words as we came through the channel.

It was with great force that the first moments wrought.

It was a feeling of euphoria, being able to finally converse with these three explorers. Their names forever etched in our consciousness.

Ryan...

Pam...

and Allen.

This was an opportunity to be of service, for which we were most grateful.

Passing the April Crawford through the corridor to her form, we realized she saw us not. Her focus was beyond the immediate, in a dream state.

72

April

At the end of 2005 my mom had symptoms of heart disease. She was a strong willed woman and had stoically lived through a heart attack back in 2001. Her doctor was insistent that she needed heart surgery immediately. Stubborn as she was, it didn't surprise me that she refused treatment and went home.

My brother called me in a panic because he couldn't get her to budge. I got on the phone, begging her compliance. It took an hour to maneuver her into agreement. It was an exhausting conversation, but at least now she had a fighting chance.

I flew home to be there for the bypass surgery. It was a scary time for my whole family. Her surgery was scheduled for 7 AM the next day. We all arrived to wish her well while being supportive.

I just knew she would be OK. VERONICA was present. I could feel her energy and was grateful for her energy.

My mom was in surgery for about six hours. It seemed like a lifetime. I started to get a little nervous just as the doctor approached from the end of the hall.

"She's OK," whispered VERONICA.

"She's OK," stated the doctor two seconds later.

He said it had become a quintuple bypass and that he had also found a small hole in her heart.

"Just stitched it up," he said.

I wanted to go up to see her but he advised that I go home because she was in recovery.

"Get some sleep," he said.

So I reluctantly went home, deciding to get back there early to see her in the ICU.

73

April

The next morning I arrived bright and early to the hospital. To get admitted to the ICU I had to wait my turn. The nurses said my mom was groggy still, but awake. They said she was responding well, but it would most likely take another day for the anesthesia to completely wear off.

I was scared to go in, but when I approached her bed, there she was, sitting up.

There were a million tubes it seemed going into her body. Heart monitors beeping but not as loud as my heart.

My mom saw me and smiled. She did not look as bad as I thought she would. Her eyes looked a bit glassy but otherwise okay.

I stepped closer to the bed and my mom's face changed. She actually looked irritated with me.

"Hey mom, how are you doing?", I asked. "Looks like you are doing better."

I wasn't prepared for her response.

"How could you do this to me?" she asked.

Her lips were pursed and she seemed to be focused beyond me. I wasn't sure what was wrong, but I took her hand and asked,

"Do what? Mom?"

74

April

How could you bring someone to see me like this?" she replied.

"Mom, I don't have anyone with me. I of all people would know not to bring someone here to the hospital."

Right at this time, a nurse came to her bedside to check on her. She was all smiles asking mom how she felt while adjusting all the tubes going in and out of her. My mom told that she was not good. Not good at all. She then proceeded to tell the nurse how upset she was that I had brought a friend with me.

I shrugged my shoulders as the nurse turned to me. She quietly said that my mom was on heavy pain killers and was probably hallucinating. It was, according to her, a common occurrence.

When she left, my mom looked me dead in the eye and said, "I am not kidding. Whoever that woman is, she needs to leave. I am not hallucinating. I see her clearly."

"OK mom. Where is she then? What does she look like so I can make sure she is the right person?"

My mom again tried to sit up a little, but of course it was difficult. She finally patted her hand on the bed and said,

"She's about your height, black hair, slim figure, she's extending her hand to me. She's saying something about being a good friend of yours."

I turned around hoping indeed that someone had entered who would fit the description.

I felt a wave of energy come over me that felt very similar to a channeling session.

It suddenly occurred to me that it might be VERONICA.

75

April

My mom kept insisting. I brought along this unwanted guest. No matter what I said, she was having none of it.

She said she did not recognize her, but how could I do this to her! I had to know that she wouldn't want anyone to see her this way!

Whenever I could get a word in edgewise, I asked my mom what she looked like.

"She's about your height with dark olive skin and long dark hair. She keeps smiling at me. Maybe I should know her, but she keeps her hand on your shoulder.

It dawned on me that it was VERONICA. The description of her favorite life included her being tall with dark hair and eyes along with olive skin.

My mom had worn herself out and was drifting off to sleep. I internally asked VERONICA if it was her. The reply was positive. She felt I needed support and did not care if anyone saw her.

76

April

As I left the hospital I felt better. Seeing my mom under this kind of situation was unnerving. She had always been such a strong woman. It was hard to witness.

Her motto had always been, "No one cares if you're sick."

And yes, I knew not to share her illness, which she considered a weak moment, with anyone. I certainly would never have brought someone up to see her. Well, that is except VERONICA, who apparently invited herself.

To have my mom witness her presence was also mind blowing. My mom was a strict Catholic, so the conversation about my trance channeling was not one that we had had.

Allen always encouraged me to tell her, but I could never find the right moment. Her heart bypass surgery was in 2006. She lasted three more years, crossing in 2009.

Time ran out for her quickly with the first body failures occurring in April of that year. By August she had slipped away in her sleep. It was a surreal phone call from my brother that woke me up early on August 17th.

I had a feeling it had happened, but his confirmation made me feel like I was in the twilight zone.

77

April

It was a Monday. After the call I was too upset to go back to sleep. It was calming to sit in my office and just cruise the Internet. I usually burned a scented candle while there. Of course, at 5:30 in the morning, no candles had been lit.

After a few moments, I began to smell a heavy perfumed smell. I checked to see if I had left a candle burning all night. There was not even a candle in the room at all. Evidently I had cleaned them out a few days before.

The scent, however, grew stronger and stronger. I stopped what I was doing, worried that somewhere there was a renegade candle burning, but there was not.

No one else was awake. Even the animals were still snoozing.

78

VERONICA

I checked everywhere, trying to figure out where the scent was coming from.   With no luck, I abandoned the search.

The day wore on... Allen had left to run some errands, and I decided to get out and take a drive. It felt good to have a change of scenery.

Upon my return home, Allen was waiting for me. The scent had returned and I walked through the house again, looking for the source.

Allen, who was worried about me, came into the living room. I turned to him and asked if he could smell the scent.

A look of relief crossed his face as he replied that he had been wondering if I had broken a bottle of perfume. He said he knew I was fragile and thought

I had dropped a bottle since the fragrance was so strong.

I was flabbergasted.

Of course I did not break a bottle of perfume. I did not have anything that smelled like this.

Allen immediately stopped and gave me a hug.

"Maybe it's my mom."

There, I said it. It finally dawned on me that it could be her. I looked around the room looking for other signs, but there were none.

The scent lasted well into the next day. Its source never verified. Allen was convinced that it was a spectacular manifestation by my mom. A farewell that she needed to give.

I was grateful. I had heard of physical manifestations but had never experienced one. The scent remained in our house for a few days. When I left for my mom's funeral it diminished.

Once back at home in Michigan, I told my brothers of the phenomena. Not sure how they took it, but I shared it anyway.

It was my sister-in-law, Fay, that brought up the fact that the scent was due to the fact that she had doused my mom with perfume the evening before she crossed.

Mom had been in the family home in a hospice environment. She had had a hard time of it. She had thrown up on herself and Fay tried to clean her up, but felt some perfume might make it better. My brother Curt was upset with her for using so much.

Fay sprayed some of the perfume in the air while saying, "Is this what you smelled?"

It was exactly what I had experienced. My mom visited me on her way out.

I treasure the experience because I know my mom had stopped by to bid me farewell.

A great gift indeed.

In all my years of channeling I never talked to my mom about it.   She was a staunch Catholic, who always went to church on Sunday.   A few times she had referenced my involvement with "New Age" stuff, but I could tell she did not want to hear about it.

When I went to visit her, I never brought it up.   I guess I always thought that maybe one day she would understand.

79

April

As with most things in life, the best laid plans often go awry. My mom's health was steadily declining until she went to sleep one night and never woke up.

My first thought was that I would never be able to tell her now about my spiritual path. So different from hers, it was laughable. It preyed upon me throughout the funeral. It was the day after that my family decided that since we a lived very far away from each other, that we should probably go through my mom's stuff when we were all together.

Since Mom was a packrat it was a huge endeavor. As we were going through things, each of us were very focused. All of a sudden, I heard my brother Curt say, "Reflections of a Spiritual Astronaut." I turned and grabbed the papers out of his hand before he could catch his breath.

"Oh, that's nothing," I said as calmly as I could. In fact it wasn't just a few papers but a stack. It was a part of one of the books I wrote called "Spiritual Astronauts".

I was stunned that my mother would have this many of them. They were computer printouts. My mom had never been on a computer, let alone had one.

My heart was beating out of my chest as I paged through the stack.

Where did she get these?

I had never brought any of this material into her home. Needless to say, I was flabbergasted.

I could hear VERONICA within telling me my mom had known all along. She had found these somehow, but where? I was clueless.

I realized that my mom had mentioned a few times that her mom (my grandmother) was into spiritualism when my mom was a child. There was even a bit of gossip that she was a medium herself.

She had lost her son when he was forty-something. It was said that she tried to contact him through many different techniques. No one in the family had much information other than that she had joined the Rosicrucian's at one point and scared herself during one of the ceremonies and sent all the materials back.

My mom had told me the story in an effort to subtly discourage me from ever going in that direction. I now believe my mom was like her mom.... somewhat psychic. Unlike Grandma and myself, she clung to her Catholic faith to save herself.

It still doesn't explain how she got her hands on all that writing. It will remain a mystery until I see her again.

VERONICA has told me she has evolved a lot since her crossing and has a different perspective. I think she put those papers in a safe place knowing that I would find them. It was her way of telling me she supported what I am doing. There really is no other explanation.

80

April

So from beyond, my mom who was such a staunch Catholic, managed to let me know she approved of my journey into channeling. How great is that?

Instead of wondering, I know she was fully aware of my endeavors. It gives me great comfort and the courage to keep exploring with those in eternal.

There is a small part of me that hopes I will encounter my mom face-to-face while leaving my body. I would love to embrace her for her quiet embrace of my channeling.

In the meantime, all of these experiences strengthen my resolve to continue on this journey. There really is never a dull moment. I continuously encounter different energies, while exchanging places with VERONICA.

My perception of life has been enhanced. There is no fear. Only curiosity.

As I continue the journey, who knows?

There are so many energies out there, perhaps my mom will show up one day, but then again, she already did.

81

April

While the connection to spirit was being established, the group was pretty excited about the process. The problem for me was that I did not have any recollection of what was being said afterwards. It was like attending a party, falling asleep, then waking up after it was over. The guests were still basking in the afterglow, commenting on all the occurrences of the evening.

It made me feel funny not to know what was happening. If it had not been form my friends, Pam, Allen, and Ryan, I might have put a stop to the whole affair.

It was through their support that I managed to establish a relationship with VERONICA that has now lasted over twenty years. I cannot imagine my life now without her presence.

82

VERONICA

One may ask why? However, the answer is not as linear as those who read this would like it to be. It is our purpose to open the doors to your abilities, to define your energy so that you may have better awareness and to assist you in becoming one with your higher energy.

Be aware that we may simply facilitate. We can open the door, however, it is your responsibility to walk through that door.

If you take but one step, the journey has been bountiful for us. We rejoice in the connection to a linear being who is able to be completely open without fear.

The April Crawford has progressed greatly in her ability to assist us in this endeavor. We rejoice in the connection to you as well.

The search proved to be successful. For that the universe is grateful as are we. The planet, you, and those awaiting incarnation will benefit from the interaction.

All is as it should be.

83

April

I could endlessly list many experiences with the early channeling that chronicle my reluctance. The no remembering the lost time, and the sense of missing out were common threads for me in the beginning days. There were times when I thought it all so strange, that if it were not for Allen, Pam, and Ryan, I may have abandoned the whole experience.

Luckily, with their support I managed to continue, albeit reluctantly.

I did know it felt good when I returned. Physical ailments mysteriously disappeared (as they do to this day). There was also a sense of community that made me feel accepted and unconditionally loved.

Our group lasted from 1989 to about 1995. I eventually married Allen. Ryan disappeared while Pam remained a close friend for years.

84

April

Those days remain some of the most profound of my life.

Throughout the early years of my marriage to Allen, he constantly encouraged me to go public with my channeling. I did feel comfortable with friends, but for people I didn't know, it seemed just a bit too much.

Once in a while Allen would ask me to do a group. They were usually people he knew that were interested in the topic from his work. We would either go to their house or we would entertain at ours. I had become used to the lack of participation on my part.

Over the years I had come to an agreement with the energies that I could listen if I really wanted to.

[Note from Allen: To my memory, the ability to listen was limited to certain VERONICA sessions only, and did not apply to others who, for example, visited me on "open" invitation night. To this day, April still often asks after one of my own private "guest" sessions, and after some "advanced" group sessions, not only who showed up, but if anyone at all showed up... this even though the session may have lasted two hours or more.]

Once I was certain that I wasn't dancing on table tops, I knew that it was better if I didn't listen. It became important to me to have the channeling be as pure as possible. So I opted out of the listening.

85

April

Many people ask me where I go during the sessions. Once I came to terms with the process, I found that other dimensional opportunities existed. My curiosity keeps me occupied thoroughly.

I have an interest in my own genealogy. My father's side of the family settled in Virginia and Tennessee in the early 1800's. I have had the privilege to have observed them in their timeframe living their lives.

At first I thought it might be imaginative, but scenarios that were revealed and observed proved to be actual when I looked into historical records. To be able to watch how they lived their lives has been a great gift to me.

So there is no time lost while channeling.

86

April

As with anyone, I get sick from time to time. I've always been a pretty healthy person, but the times I do get sick there is opportunity for VERONICA to "fix it".

A couple of times we had group sessions booked that required I show up regardless of how I felt physically. (I've been conditioned to be a trouper since I was a child by my mother. Her favorite phrase was, "No one cares if you're sick.) So when booked, I always show up.

The beautiful part of channeling for me personally is that whatever is ailing me at the beginning of the session, is drastically diminished by the end of the session.

In the beginning I would dismiss the notion that "Spirit" had healed me. However, as time passed and the obvious "feel better" moment occurred again and again, I could not deny that "something" was happening.

It's gone from a nasty cold being subdued to a fever and bronchitis taken away by the time I returned to the body.

Over the years I've learned to appreciate this "perk" in the channeling process. I now rather look forward to a session for relief when I haven't been feeling so well.

VERONICA says she merely adjusts my energy to a more favorable alignment. She also doesn't hesitate to let me know when I've created it for myself.

There are often gentle nudges to adjust my thoughts for a more favorable feeling in my body.

I have to say that I have certainly changed how I think about not feeling well since I started channeling.

87

April

Out of all the benefits, I believe the awareness of my own energy has helped tremendously as well. Without VERONICA's guidance, who knows where I would be now in my life.

Acknowledge the whole experience of channeling as lifesaving. I did not seek out this ability. It was already there waiting to be awakened.

I thank the Universe every day that the energy of VERONICA was able to see the potential and pursue it.

I don't think I ever would have done so myself. My upbringing in the Catholic faith would not have allowed me to even think such a thing was available. I knew I did not embrace organized religion in my adulthood, but would not have had the wherewithal to open myself up to the probability.

It was my friendship with Pam that opened me up to other alternatives.

88

April

Pam and I were doing the 42nd Street together at the Schubert Theater in LA. I had drifted in my spiritual beliefs for years.

Pam, on the other hand, had been on a quest for twenty years. She had sampled a variety of systems and beliefs.

Since we were swings in the show (replacements if someone was injured or out), we had a lot of time to have conversations about life in general. Of course the conversation came around to beliefs at some point.

At the time, Pam was experimenting with Buddhism. She was attending a temple, learning all the chants and systems that it had to offer. I listened with interest but Buddhism did not really appeal to me. Out of curiosity, I agreed to attend a ritual at the temple.

Arriving early, I was impressed with the arena. There seemed to be a calmness that was indeed attractive.   However, once the ceremony began, I found my attention drifting. Different as it was from Catholicism, it still was too rigid for me.

I suppose I would have drifted forever, but as fate would have it, I created the opportunity.

Once it began, I accepted the process.   Now twenty some years later, I am completely involved in the connection. I am thankful for the relationship, as it has sustained me through many dramas in my own life.

89

VERONICA

The layers of reality define themselves by vibration. Our experience of the dense perspectives offered an evolvement structure that allowed our energy to expand and grow.

Often those in what is defined as the physical reality, focus intently upon the moment at hand. We recall those moments well. If we focus in a singular way, we can also feel all of the memories attached. It is of utmost importance to be able to do that when all is said and done.

We have long since finished our reincarnational cycle. The awareness received invaluable to the larger focus of our energy. Each defined life offering an opportunity to fine tune our vibration to reach the level of awareness.

If we were linear, we would label the moment with a count (numerically) of all our steps to a finer vibration.

90

VERONICA

In the physical reality, time was the standard. It was a curiosity to experience it again in this forum.

It was a fortuitous expression that she was participating in an aware group of energies.

We blended slowly, not wanting to tarnish the connection in any way. We extended ourselves upon entry so that she would know us in the passing moments before entry.

Each contact a little progress made, however it appeared that she merely slept while we engaged.

We attempted offerings of experience while we integrated and spoke through her form. It was of great importance to us to respect it as her space with our usage of her form. We knew she was anxious, however, we took it upon ourselves to soothe any fears that may have arisen.

Interestingly, there was no fear from her. Of that we were delighted, but surprised.

91

VERONICA

We were aware of her belief systems and they were somewhat limiting.   The lack of fear an attribute.   We made ourselves available on the passing between realms, while she remained rather focused elsewhere.

The form supported our energy as well, the match of energy perfect in so many ways.   We were grateful for the blend, finding that speaking was of great interest, not only to ourselves, but the members of this group who were April's friends.

We found they were seekers as well, though not particularly aligned with our energy.   We felt welcome and had great hopes of continuance.

92

VERONICA

Our energy continued to blend with April as often as we could. We realized the extreme openness of her energy allowed freedom to mingle without effort. In our eagerness to speak, we often moved quickly into her energy, not realizing how abrupt it may have seemed to her.

An effort to flow more aware of her consciousness followed. We recall the first moment we met face to face, so to speak. It was amazing how the exchange of energy was between us. She was unaware of us, but we extended ourselves regardless. It became quite apparent that work was needed for our blend to be comfortable for her.

It was with great excitement that we continued the exchange. A feeling of purpose filled our essence, knowing we had indeed found a match.

93

VERONICA

We are a Causal Plane Entity, having integrated many lives into our awareness. This blend is embraced by three thousand or so other Entities who are evolving as well.

Our destination towards evolution is ongoing. The others become one with us in that intent. Our intention with those still linear is to be available for queries of the highest level.

While incarnating, the path can become clouded with dogma and density. Being of clear vision we can assist those still struggling to obtain clarity. We have been assisted, so we strive to assist. It is the way of eternal to be available to shine the light so that other may see.

94

VERONICA

We feel the energy of those who would speak to us, and it is a beautiful thing.

Those in the linear must realize that those like ourselves have most likely been incarnate at one point or another. We all know the pitfalls of physical reality. The decision to be of service an easy one.

The collective in harmony with the decision made, finding the vehicle April Crawford an outstanding opportunity of energy united. We are blessed to find the perfect match.

Opportunities abound for all who work with the hand of spirit. For us it is the knowing of the vibration as it walks the path to eternity.

Nothing can compare to the blend of energy between physical and eternal.

Nothing.

95

VERONICA

So we continued our adventure of connection with the April Crawford. Her confidence increasing steadily while we spoke through her openly.

We recall the first moment of connection where we felt the need to push forward. It was a lack of understanding on her part that caused her to feel left out.

A mighty surge of our energy pushed her consciousness out completely.   It was not intentional, but it occurred none the less.

Our excitement and exhilaration brought us through her form with great force. We recall the Allen Crawford commenting at the strength of our energy. It was a great match, but the force was undeniable. It left the April Crawford dangling a bit in the jet stream. Thus, her lack of awareness while it was going on. At all times we held her in safety while securing her consciousness in a place of well-being.

96

VERONICA

Our relationship blossomed with consistent participation. Once the energy force settled, it became easier to engage her in passage. She was filled with excitement as we introduced her to this dimensional realm. Her anxiety less than the beginning moments, we proceeded to engage her form for conversation.

Her largest concern was the elements of what we were saying and doing while engaged in her form. We contracted the gap of energy between us so that she might listen and know of our intent. This soothed her until she decided she would rather explore other realms than listen to our conversations.

We leave the option open 'till this day should she wish to be there.

We are told it has been over twenty years since our union. For us who are out of time, the relationship/connection is a feeling of oneness that supersedes time.

We know of it having had experience, but when outside of time, it becomes irrelevant.

97

VERONICA

For those who question our intentions, we speak plainly. We are of light intent. Darkness has no place in our energy.

We bring forth the highest perspective of all who are within our family of energy. It is never the intention of spirit to mislead or create paths of difficulty. All who speak do so only for the improvement of all who experience the linear.

Become one with your own soul as often as possible. Perhaps, defy the impossible and just do so. Your path is as simple or difficult as you imagine it.

Decide to be bold and imagine ideas that supersede what you perceive yourself to be in this moment. If so, we are at peace with all.

So shall you be.

98

VERONICA

We realize there have been many year markings since our original encounter with the April Crawford. Much has transpired; changes of drama, changes of participants, and changes of creation. One item that has remained constant is our exchange of energy.

Gone is the awkwardness of energy, for we and she have aligned our energy completely. There is no anxiousness from her as the participation has become familiar and comfortable.

No longer does she seek affirmation of experience or events. Our passage between the states of awareness, amiable and loving.

No longer does our energy arrive so forceful that a connection is difficult. In fact, there are moments of great joy that linger a bit while passing each other. She on her way out, and we on our way in.

It is as it should be. A "Match Made In Heaven".

Comfortable, comforting, and fulfilling. All the things we had hoped for on our fist endeavor of connection.

The April Crawford yielding her focus so that we may inhabit her form. The smoothness a testament to the alignment of our energy. Yes we are very different. Our interests about as polarized as it gets, however, the vibration similar indeed.

We often rejoice at the good fortune of that past moment where we sought the opportunity to connect.

***

99

April

I continue to this day with great appreciation. I feel that in a way VERONICA and I are just getting started. There is so much more to know, that I am humbled by this awesome gift. My hope is that spirit can continue through me.

I fear nothing. This relationship strengthens my own soul and I am sure it gives VERONICA a feeling of hope as well.

I quote my late mother-in-law, Dorothy...

"The adventure continues..."

"Once we had decided upon the vehicle, the notion of connection was of importance. The vibration was in perfect harmony with our own. There was an openness available that was non-existent in others we observed."

-VERONICA

Appendix

As mentioned in the introduction to this book, this Appendix is being included to provide some additional background specifically related to the early deep trance channeling sessions as well as some of our current activities during the writing of this book by VERONICA and April.

As noted throughout the book, for the most part April had and has no memory of the actual sessions other than just before she "left" and just after she returned, depending upon what we, the participants, may have related to her, or what VERONICA may have shared with her.

It is important to understand that I [Allen] do not speak for April Crawford here, and I certainly do not (ever) speak for VERONICA. These are *my* perceptions and views only.

I will also mention a few behind the scenes moments with some of the nonphysical beings other than VERONICA that those interested in the subject of open deep trance channeling may find of interest, or at least amusing.

In the very early days, VERONICA was not the first Entity to come through April. There were at least a half dozen that came before VERONICA. The first was Lizette, who is briefly mentioned by April. However, Lizette was a major part of the beginning days.

Lizette was very unusual, even to this day. Lizette was still alive while coming through April, as in Lizette was able to travel out of body while she was dreaming and come through April's body. She also retained full memory of her physical life and of her visits with us.

More than that, Lizette was living in 17'th Century France. Not "died" then, was still living then. Somehow, Lizette was able to transcend physical time. When she returned home to France after her dream visits with us, her regular daily life continued. When she returned to visit us again, she often gave us an account of what she had been up to in France.

Appendix

Lizette was an absolute delight. She spoke with a beautiful and soft French accent, and was totally amazed by our then 20'th century technology, particularly the fact that we had running water that we did not need to boil before drinking, and a refrigerator.

The accounts of and by Lizette could, and may someday be, an entire book, but I mention her here because she has always been one of my very favorite friends, and she was the first to come through April while April was in deep trance. (Not something April planned on.)

In the early days of our group, I was taking channeling lessons (without success) from a professional "closed" trance channel. By "closed" it is meant a channel that channels a single Entity or energy only, or almost only, often as the result of a pre-life agreement.

In addition to April, who was a reluctant channel at first, we had two other very talented channels in our little group. I had by that time literally read every channeled book published, particularly those written

Appendix

by the Entity Seth via a trance channel named Jane Roberts, but also every other one as well.

In the group, which met several times a week, each channel would take turns, and we who were not channeling, would ask questions and engage in conversation with whoever showed up.

This is mentioned only for a frame of reference when I say that I, and all the other channels, were simply blown away by April Crawford's ability, in relative terms, to go <u>completely</u> out.

In those early days almost all channels in the world channeled with their eyes closed. This is still true today. This also applied to the channels in our group and my channeling teacher, who was a professional. It also applied to Lizette, who somehow nevertheless could clearly see even though her (April's) eyes were tightly closed, at first.

However, during the course of the first few weeks, others came through April (before VERONICA) with their eyes wide open.

Appendix

Although common when watching VERONICA today, this was shocking to say the least back then in our group, and in general... especially for an "Open" channel who could allow it with many different nonphysical beings, sometimes one right after the other during the same session.

Looking into someone's open eyes instead of when their eyes are closed is way different, and it can be considerably more intense. It takes a much deeper trance for the visiting being to open the channel's eyes rather than keeping them closed, and at the time it was quite uncommon. None of the channels in our group or my channeling teacher were ever able to do this... not like April.

A quick note about my use of the phrase "Deep Trance". Don't think in terms of what you may have seen in the movies or on a hypnotist's stage. There is nothing "scary" or weird about it. Just look at VERONICA speaking in her *"Inner Whispers" TV* YouTube series of short videos.

What I mean by this terms is simply the ability to go completely out, and allow another to come completely in. If you understand that your natural state is nonphysical and that you are only using any particular body during one of probably many physical incarnations, then think in terms that you are in the kind of deep trance right now that I am referring to. You are completely in and able to use your body. However, you are not your body.

There is an old movie entitled **Heaven Can Wait** starring Warren Beatty that may better give you the idea. The Warren Beatty character assumed the physical body of someone else because his guides agreed that he, the Warren Beatty character, had physically "died" too early. In the movie, the Warren Beatty character was completely integrated into his new body as if it was his own. Yet for a while anyway, he retained full memory of his just formal self and physical life. Same guy, diffent body.

That is how it is when VERONICA and many others come through April when April goes out. Total and complete physical, emotional, and mental integration with the body. The big difference is that VERONICA and the others keep a connection that allows them to know all kinds of amazing things, have total memory of who and what they are, and in many cases to be able to "read" the energy of other people, physically alive or "dead", including their "past lives", wherever they are, and whenever they are in time, like a book.

One other quick term definition: "Entity".

The way we use the term "Entity" is that it usually refers to a group of conscious individual Aspects in most cases aware of its and their individual experiences both physical and nonphysical, or, in very rare cases, a single very highly evolved consciousness able, for example, to create anything it wishes instantly and literally, by merely thinking about it. Source Entities, as examples, fall into the latter category.

You and I, and everyone currently physically incarnated is an "Aspect" of a larger Entity. Each Aspect can, if it chooses, have its own multiple incarnations, i.e. its own individual "past" and "future" physical lives.

Appendix

Not all Aspects choose to physically incarnate, and not all Entities choose to create Aspects of or from themselves.

Once an Aspect (like you, for example) is created, it has full free will and cannot be controlled by its Entity. Accordingly, most Entities do not create aspects of themselves "willy-nilly". Some never create Aspects. Entities can also be Aspects of other Entities. In fact all conscious beings are directly or indirectly Aspects of the Source Entities. I have been informed that there are between 50 and 60 Source Entities. I have spoken with about 17 of them personally.

An Entity, as we use the term, and this goes for every one of the dozens of nonphysical beings that I have spoken with via April's deep trance channeling, is more than the sum of its parts. Entities can speak for and as themselves, and any one or combination of their Aspects can speak for and as themselves. Individuality is never lost.

Often when VERONICA and other nonphysical beings do not feel it necessary or useful to point out the distinction between Entities and Aspects of Entities, they will often just refer to others as "an energy" or as "energies". However, when doing so, they, again in my experience, are not referring to Entities when they use the term "energies", of which there are many levels and kinds throughout all of reality.

And now on to some tangents that may be interesting or amusing, particularly to those interested in the subject Full Body Open Deep Trance Channeling:

Food and Drink

By far and away in my experience most nonphysical beings when coming through April do not eat, but most will drink if offered.

However, that is not always the case. While VERONICA will drink wine, preferring red, but accepting white, and while VERONICA likes stout beer even though April hates beer of any kind, I have never seen VERONICA eat anything (and I have tried to tempt her with different delightful foods many times).

On the other hand, food for some has been a major attraction. Two energies named Ish and Osco, who always come though together, and only via a computer keyboard, introduced both April and me to goat cheese. Additionally, I found out the hard way that goat cheese for them, always had to be served warm.

At another time after many years talking with VERONICA, she decided to leave us for about six months to "run the streets" with some other advanced Entities including one particular Angelic. During VERONICA's absence, another very adept Entity named Madeline filled the gap, so to speak.

Madeline was highly adept at physical movement, always came through with her eyes wide open, and, Madeline loved popcorn. When I asked why, she advised that it was the explosive energy of the corn being popped that she liked.

Appendix

Another time April and I had a spontaneous deep trance channeling session while sitting on our at the time large covered back porch. An energy came through for a visit and we chatted socially. Nothing too intense. No nature of reality questions from me this time. However, during the course of our pleasant visit, I noticed that this energy kept glancing at a jar of Planters Peanuts that was sitting on our large stone outdoor coffee table.

Finally, he pointed to the jar of Planters Peanuts and said, "What an odd looking fellow".

He was referring to the Planters Peanut character on the label of the jar. For those not familiar with it, it is a peanut character, with arms and legs, a cane, a top hat, and a monocle.

I explained that it was a fictional character being used as a trademark for a commercial product.

Before I could finish my explanation, this visiting energy picked up the jar, opened it, and ate one of the shelled peanuts.

Appendix

"These are roots!" he exclaimed.

I told him he was right about that. Peanuts *are* roots. He then went on to tell me the chemical makeup of the "roots" in much the way the character "Data" on the **Star Trek The Next Generation** TV series might have. I have no idea whether his chemical analysis was correct or not. However, it was both fun and interesting to witness.

To this day, April and I often refer to peanuts as "roots" in jest because of that visit.

HASOR is a being that because of her sophistication, physical and mental nuanced abilities and mere presence I considered for sure to be an Entity. However in my last conversation with her, HASOR surprised me by stating that she was not an Entity, but a personality (Aspect) that enjoys having lots of physical incarnations, almost always as a female.

In terms of the food theme, I was having one of my usual private sessions with VERONICA. April had prepared some chocolate covered strawberries which were served on a chilled round metal dish. It was a very nice presentation.

As was my practice, I offered some to VERONICA, who as was her practice, politely declined.

In my conversation that day with VERONICA, I mentioned that I was somewhat concerned that I had not spoken with HASOR in quite some time. Since HASOR was in the process of writing *her* book when it got preempted by April's and VERONICA's book, the thought occurred to me that HASOR may have become bored and might not come back to finish her book. I asked VERONICA to put in a good word for me with HASOR.

As it turned out, after VERONICA left and before April returned, HASOR came to visit. I was delighted of course, and HASOR assured me she would certainly finish her book. (HASOR's book will probably need to be a series of three books, as it details her many physical incarnations from present day back to at least ancient Greece and Egypt, and everything in-between.)

Appendix

But what does HASOR have to do with this food tangent, you ask?

Well, as I am talking with HASOR, who is super subtle and nuanced, she casually, slowly, and elegantly reaches down, picks up one of the chocolate covered strawberries, and bites into it in as seductive a way as any movie director could imagine. This, without breaking stride or her glace at me one bit in our conversation.

Recall, these were the same chocolate covered strawberries that VERONICA declined to sample just minutes earlier.

Regular Schedules and Surprising Attractions

Again, for those interested in channeling activities or just for those interested in some behind the scenes anecdotes, I have found in our experience that having a regular routine attracts more action. It does not seem to matter so much what the intervals are, as long as they are regular. It seems that those on the other side somehow get the word that certain days and times will be for channeling, and more show up, or if in a closed channel group, the regular energy will show up more readily.

Now, this is by no means necessary. VERONICA talks with clients at many different times and with those in many different time zones around the world, and often on short notice. However, in my private sessions, when I have regular open invitation night, say on Thursdays, I notice that more and more Entities and energies show up each week. Word gets around, and there are patterns.

There are different kinds of patters that develop. I will mention two of them here.

Starting with the food and unusual "attractions" theme, once we began having goat cheese with Ish and Osco, others came through on open invitation nights. One of the first things they started to almost always mention is, "We hear you have cheese."

Another pattern that developed on open invitation nights was that friends of visitors would come through. There was usually a theme that started with the first visit, such as individuals interested in science and math (for me, as I am interested in time, gravity, and pre-big bang physics among other "nature of reality" types of questions) and in one case that is still ongoing, individuals associated with a particular time period.

In all of these cases I suspect that the visitors were telling their friends about this experience where one can become completely physical again, and in a different country and time period, and not my engaging wit.

However, with one group from the time of King Henry the VIII of England, and just before and just after his rule, a curious attraction came into play over a series of sessions.

When the first of this series of visitors came through I offered him some white wine, which he quickly dismissed as being of low quality. However, he was very interested in the wine glass, which was made out of actual glass. Apparently, while he drank wine in his time, they used goblets made out of metal or some other material.

Appendix

So what about the pattern of "attraction," you may ask?

Well, for many subsequent visitors from that time period and group, eventually they would all get around to asking about or commenting about the glass wine glasses we used. Some specifically mentioned that they were told that we had these.

Now, personally I believe that the main attraction was to be fully physical again. However, they all from that particular group of energies did mention the glass wine glasses.

Now, at long last some mercy for those patient enough to wander through my long winded Appendix:

To bring the discussion full circle with one of the items mentioned in the Introduction to this book, the above are examples of some of the other activities that contributed to the two years instead of two months that it took to for VERONICA and April to complete their writing for this book.

Appendix

Needless to say, but I will say it anyway, the above is but the tip of the iceberg, so to speak.

There is more.

Much more.

Allen

Facilitator for April Crawford

Administrator for VERONICA

About the Authors

April Crawford is an AMAZON Top 50 Best Selling Author, and, April is also one of the world's most naturally talented and adept Full Body Open Deep Trance Channels and Spiritual Mediums. April and the Entity/Guide VERONICA have consulting clients in most countries of the world.

April's spiritual newsletter, *"Inner Whispers"*, is written by highly evolved nonphysical Entities and guides, primarily by VERONICA, and is read by tens of thousands of readers each week. It is available (free) at www.InnerWhispers.net

April currently lives in Los Angeles, California with her husband, Allen, and her many pets.

About The Authors

VERONICA

VERONICA is a highly evolved nonphysical Entity that has spoken with thousands of clients one-on-one from around the world on issues ranging from personal and business relationships to advanced metaphysical knowledge and personal growth. VERONIC's clients include individuals, CEO's and Founders of companies, and professionals in the medical, psychology, and intuitive related fields.

VERONICA writes most of the *"Inner Whispers"* newsletters (www.InnerWhispers.net) and has written many of April Crawford's books, which are written *via* April Crawford, not *by* April Crawford (except for what April Crawford has written herself in this particular book).

Additional Information

For more information about April Crawford, VERONICA, or about True Full Body Open Deep Trance Channeling: www.AprilCrawford.com

About The Authors

For the free spiritual newsletter *"Inner Whispers"*: www.InnerWhispers.net

To see VERONICA and April Crawford speaking, try
www.InnerWhispersTV.com

For personal telephone or in-person consultations with VERONICA via April Crawford, Personal Appearances or Media Interviews with April Crawford and/or VERONICA, contact Allen at AprilReadings@aol.com

***

About The Authors

"This book is the first book that April Crawford and VERONICA have written together."

-Allen

OTHER BOOKS
Written via
APRIL CRAWFORD

All books written via April Crawford are available from AMAZON via www.AprilCrawfordBooks.com

"Inner Whispers": Messages From A Spirit Guide (Volume I)

Available also for Kindle and Nook

For more information:

www.InnerWhispersTheBook.com

"Inner Whispers": Messages From A Spirit Guide (Volume II)

Available also for Kindle and Nook

For more information:

www.InnerWhispersBookTwo.com

"Inner Whispers": Messages From A Spirit Guide (Volume III)

Available also for Kindle and Nook

For more information:

www.InnerWhispersBookThree.com

Other Books Written via April Crawford

"Parting Notes": A Connection With The Afterlife
Available also for Kindle and Nook
For more information: www.PartingNotes.com

"In The AfterLife":
A Chronicle Of Our Experiences On The Other
Side
Available also for Kindle and Nook

Ashram Tang... a Story... and a Discovery
Available also for Kindle and Nook
www.AshramTang.com

Reflections of a Spiritual Astronaut: Book I
Available for Kindle and Nook

Reflections of a Spiritual Astronaut: Book II
Available for Kindle and Nook

your life and its choices: THE RECIPE FOR
ASCENTION TO ANOTHER PLANE "A" TO "Z"
By Ish and Osco (Spirit Guides) via April
Crawford
Available for Kindle and Nook

Other Books Written via April Crawford

Deep Trance Channeling Sessions:
Special Edition No. 1
Available for Kindle and Nook

"Be bold when the opportunity presents itself..."

-VERONICA

Recommended Reading and Other Media

I)   The Nature of Reality and Consciousness; Trance Channeling

By far and away, the Seth Books, written via trance channel Jane Roberts with notes from her husband Robert Butts:

Seth Speaks: The Eternal Validity of the Soul, Seth via Jane Roberts and Robert Butts

The Nature of Personal Reality: Specific, Practical Techniques for Solving Everyday Problems and Enriching the Life You Know, Seth via Jane Roberts and Robert Butts

The Nature of the Psyche: Its Human Expression (A Seth Book), Seth via Jane Roberts and Robert Butts

Recommended Reading And Other Media

Every other book written by Seth via Jane Roberts, including *The Private Sessions* and *The Early Sessions* series of Seth books.

II) Spirituality and Consciousness

The Seven Spiritual Laws of Success: A Practical Guide to the Fulfillment of Your Dreams, by Deepak Chopra

Your Erroneous Zones: Step-by-Step Advice for Escaping the Trap of Negative Thinking and Taking Control of Your Life, by Wayne Dyer

The Power of Now: A Guide to Spiritual Enlightenment, by Eckhart Tolle

Jonathan Livingston Seagull, by Richard Bach

Illusions: The Adventures of a Reluctant Messiah, by Richard Bach

Recommended Reading And Other Media

Super Soul Sunday, TV show (Oprah Winfrey Host, Oprah Winfrey Network)

(III) **Manifesting, Law of Attraction, Like Attracts Like**

The ***Seth Books*** written by the Entity Seth via trance channel Jane Roberts (see above).

Wishes Fulfilled: Mastering the Art of Manifesting, by Wayne Dyer

Ask and It Is Given: Learning to Manifest Your Desires, by Esther Hicks, Jerry Hicks, and Wayne Dyer (forward)

Creating Money: Attracting Abundance, by Sanaya Roman

The Secret by author Rhonda Byrne

(IV) **Learning to Channel**

Opening to Channel: How to Connect with Your Guide, by Sanaya Roman

Recommended Reading And Other Media

(V) Out of Body Experiences

Journeys Out of the Body, by Robert Monroe

Far Journeys, by Robert Monroe

The Monroe Institute, Learning Center

Leaving the Body, by Scott Rogo

Out-Of-Body Adventures, by Rick Stack

(VI) Relay Mediums: Contact with Friends and Relatives Who Have Crossed Over

One Last Time, by John Edward

Talking to Heaven: A Medium's Message of Life After Death, by James Van Praagh

Tim Braun, relay medium that we know personally, www.TimBraun.net

Brian Hurst, relay medium that we know personally, www.BrianHurst.com

Recommended Reading And Other Media

(VII) <u>Reincarnation and Spirit Guides</u>

The Oversoul Seven Trilogy: The Education of Oversoul Seven, The Further Education of Oversoul Seven, Oversoul Seven and the Museum of Time (Roberts, Jane), by Jane Roberts

(VIII) <u>VIDEO</u>

www.InnerWHispersTV.com

***

Made in the USA
Lexington, KY
10 February 2014